The Nashville Number System

by Chas Williams

Edition 7
Copyright ©1988, 1994, 1997, 2001, 2005, 2008 by Chas Williams. All rights reserved.
ISBN 0-9630906-7-4

"This is the most complete version of the *Nashville Number System* as I've ever seen. Chas Williams has a full understanding of the number system, and this book is an excellent source to begin learning the *Nashville Number System*."

- Charlie McCoy

"Finally a `How to' on the *Nashville Number System*! What used to be inside information in the studios of Music City USA is now made available to the public. Chas Williams has spent hours of intense research and interviewing to bring to you the unique art of writing music in numbers, instead of traditional manuscript. This system has saved literally hours of studio and rehearsal time in Nashville, and even across America. All I can say is thank you, Chas for an interesting, well-written, and `Timely' contribution to the music world."

- Lura Foster

"The *Nashville Number System*, by Chas Williams, is a book I really needed back in 1983 when I moved to Nashville for a recording career. I had to learn it bit by bit, trying to keep up. It can save you alot of time and embarrassing moments."

- Mark O'Connor

"This book seems to be the definitive answer to those desiring to understand the *Nashville Number System*. In addition to a brief history of the system, the book details several versions exemplifying the variety of styles used. I highly recommend it for anyone involved or seeking to become involved in the Nashville music community."

- Brent Rowan

" Chas Williams' book is as valid in Boston as in Nashville. Berklee is using the book to prepare students for the recording industry."

- Robert Stanton
Assistant Professor-Berklee College of Music

"After looking through The *Nashville Number System*, it would be in my opinion, the most informative book for learning this system and being able to apply your own way of using this method."

- Eddie Bayers

"I've hired Chas to write charts for several of my recording sessions, including John Michael Montgomery. The players on the sessions commented on how clear and precise the charts were. The explanations in Chas' book make it easy to understand the Nashville Number System. I especially like all the different versions of charts by some of my favorite players around town."

-Scott Hendricks
Producer/Engineer

Table of Contents

Introduction 1
Major Scale and Number Substitution Table 4
The Major Scale Derivation 6
    Chromatic Scale 6
    Intervals 6
    Step Formula 6
    The Major Scale and Number Substitution 6
The Nashville Numbers 8
    Assigning Chord Numbers 8
    Relative Minor 9
    Chord Symbols 10
    Chord Symbol Chart 11
Time 12
    Time Signature 12
    Common Time Signatures 12
    Note Values 12
    Rests 13
    Dotted Notes 14
    Triplets 14
    Quarter Note Triplets 14
    Tied Notes 15
    Split Bars 15
    New Time Signature 16
    Melody Notation 18
Presentation 19
    Structure 19
    Format 20
    Arranging 21
Special Instructions 22
    Tempo 22
    Count Off 22
    Pickup Notes 22
    Extra Measure 23
    Repeat Sign ‖: :‖ 23
    D.S. al Coda 24
    Vamp 24

Modulation: Mod ↗	25
Walkups and Walkdowns 5 ↗ or 1 ↘	26
Speaking Numbers In Nashville	26

Dynamics 27
Diamonds ◇	27
Bird's Eye ⌒	27
Cut Off ▲	28
Anticipation >	28
Loudness ⟩— or —⟨	28
Ritard: rit. _____	29

Feel and Style 30
4/4 Common Time	30
Straight Feel (Eighths)	30
Rock	31
Rock Eighths	31
2/4 Two Four	31
Swing	31
Shuffle	32
Rock Shuffle	32
₵ Cut Time:	33
Halftime Feel	33
3/4 Waltz	34
6/8 Halftime Waltz	35
Ballad	35
Triplet Feel	35

Common Mistakes 36

String Of Pearls • Chart Descriptions 38
1. String Of Pearls	39
2. Uncle John's Cabin	39
3. White Hardware	40
4. Perfume & Bubblegum	40
5. Claire and Calvin	41
6. Waylon	42
7. Boogie Shuffle	42
8. Winter Break	43
9. Pelican Shuffle	43
10. Amazing Grace	44

String Of Pearls • Handwritten Charts c45
    1. String Of Pearls c45
    2. Uncle John's Cabin c51
    3. White Hardware c60
    4. Perfume & Bubblegum c67
    5. Claire and Calvin c74
    6. Waylon c79
    7. Boogie Shuffle c86
    8. Winter Break c93
    9. Pelican Shuffle c99
    10. Amazing Grace c105

Chartist Bio's 111
    Charlie McCoy 111
        Charts ....**#1**-c46, **#2**-c53-54, **#7**-c87, **#8**-c94, **#10**-c106
    David Briggs 112
        Charts ....**#2**-c55-c56, **#10**-c107
    Lura Foster 112
        Charts ....**#3**-c61-62, **#4**-c69-c70, **#5**-c75-c76, **#6**-c81, **#10**-c109
    Brent Rowan 114
        Charts ....**#1**-c50, **#2**-c59, **#3**-c66, **#5**-c78, **#7**-c90
    Biff Watson 114
        Charts ....**#1**-c48, **#4**-c71, **#5**-c77, **#6**-c82, **#10**-c110
    Jimmy Capps 115
        Charts: ....**#1**-c47, **#6**-c80, **#8**-c95, **#9**-c100, **#10**-c108
    Eddie Bayers 116
        Charts ....**#3**-c65, **#6**-c84, **#7**-c92, **#8**-c98, **#9**-c104
    John Hobbs 117
        Charts ....**#1**-c49, **#3**-c63, **#4**-c72, **#7**-c89, **#8**-c96
    Chris Farren 117
        Charts ....**#4**-c73, **#6**-c85, **#9**-c102
    Tony Harrell 118
        Charts ....**#2**-c57, **#4**-c68, **#6**-c83, **#7**-c88, **#9**-c101
    Mike Chapman 118
        Charts ....**#2**-c58, **#3**-c64, **#7**-c91, **#8**-c97, **#9**-c103
    Chas Williams 119
        Charts .... **#1**-c45, **#2**-c51-c52, **#3**-c60, **#4**-c67, **#5**-c74, **#6**-c79, **#7**-c86, **#8**-c93
        #9-c99, **#10**-c105

More Handwritten Charts 120

Introduction

The *Nashville Number System* is a method of transcribing music so that a song can be understood and performed. Nashville chord charts substitute numbers for the chord letter symbols found in traditional music notation. Rhythmic and dynamic notations, as well as chord voicing symbols from formal music are used in conjunction with symbols developed uniquely by Nashville musicians.

Since the middle ages, musicians have substituted Roman numerals for chord letters. However, around 1957, **Neal Matthews**, a member of the *Jordanaires*, originated the idea of substituting regular numbers for notes. Neal said he was familiar with the system of shape notes used by gospel quartets in the 30's and 40's, which used a different shape for each note of the major scale. Working several recording sessions a day forced Neal to devise a method of writing vocal parts so that the *Jordanaires* wouldn't have to commit tremendous amounts of material to memory. He began writing vocal charts substituting numbers for the shape notes and developed his own system of writing music with numbers.

In the early 60's **Charlie McCoy** noticed the unique approach that Neal and the Jordanaires used to map out a song on paper. So, Charlie applied Neal's number system to chords and the rhythm section. Charlie was doing a lot of sessions with Wayne Moss, David Briggs, Harold Bradley, Bob Moore, Pete Wade, Ray Edenton and Grady Martin. The idea of substituting numbers for chord letters quickly spread among the other session players in Nashville. Musicians used the number system to chart out an entire song on one piece of paper while hearing a demo of the tune for the first time. This innovative number system has become the standard method of music notation in Nashville.

From a conversation with **Harold Bradley**, he said," The A team was memorizing all the stuff. One day we had a substitute; we had Wayne Moss. I looked over and Wayne had a little bitty small pad and he was writing, and Charlie McCoy was over there working with him. I went over and said, 'What are you guys doing?' They said,'Well, we're writing this down.' Charlie had studied at the University Of Miami and that's what they were doing was writing down the number system. I walked away thinking,'well what's this?' because we were used to memorizing it. But I found out when I became leader that it saved you 15 minutes a session if you could do the charts before the session. Back then, sometimes they didn't write the same chords to each verse."

Harold said,"Once, Vicki Carr came and looked over my shoulder and said, 'You guys aren't in the music business, you're in the numbers business."

"That was the only way we'd work with the Monkee's because the guy hadn't written the song. He came out after about an hour or so of us sitting around. He strummed the guitar and we wrote down the chords, and then later on he wrote the words. It was not the way we usually made music," Harold said.

One of the main benefits of a number chart is that it can be played in any key without transposing or rewriting the chart into a different key. A chart's numbers maintain their same relationship with a song's chord changes regardless of the key.

For example, if Dolly Parton sings *I Saw the Light* in the key of **C**, Johnny Cash might have sung the same song lower, in the key of **G**. If they use identical arrangements, the same Nashville number chart of *I Saw the Light* would work for both Dolly's and Johnny's performance. As well, dictation of a song from a recording or radio is easy because you don't need to know the song's key to write down the correct chord changes and melodies. This is especially nice for those of us not blessed with perfect pitch.

Over the years, country music has expanded to include more complex rhythm patterns and chord structures. Phrasing and rhythms from pop, rock, jazz, blues, cajun, and reggae have been incorporated into the music of country artists. As a result, musicians have combined traditional notation symbols with Nashville chord charts so complex music can be transcribed and played precisely. There are symbols and notations unique to the *Nashville Number System* not found anywhere else. For example, the *Diamond* ⟨5⟩ means to strike and hold a chord for the designated amount of time.

Oddly enough, there is no one definitive version of the *Nashville Number System*. Everyone use the basic Nashville concept, but many musicians use different symbols and notations to express the same musical idea. For example, a diamond may be written: ⟨5⟩ and ⋄5. Also, some people indicate a split bar (a measure with more than one chord change) with a diagonal slash: *1/5*, whereas others enclose the measure with parentheses *(15)*, or in a box 15 . Some people underline the split bar: *15* . This book explores some of the different styles and techniques of writing number charts that are used by some of the most respected musicians in Nashville.

<u>**Don't be scared**</u>. The Number System is easy. You don't have to know how to read music to learn how to write a number chart. If you flip through this book, you will see some really detailed chord charts. But, there are also some really simple bare bones charts. Apply this book to what you need. If you are a songwriter and just need to show how to follow the chords to your song, then all you need is to be able to figure out what the "1" chord is and then find the numbers for the rest of the song. After that, learn how to count the proper amount of beats for each measure and where to place each bar on the page. Once you've learned how to do all that, you'll be ready to have some musicians play your song. The players can add their own arrangement notation.

If you want to get farther into Nashville musicianship, this book will teach you some fundamental music theory and how to notate more complex rhythms. You can learn to write your chart with any degree of detail you need; a basic road map number chart, open to interpretation, or a chart with a highly detailed arrangement notation that includes the licks you have written for the song.

• Also, I describe the *Nashville Number System* **spoken language**. Whenever there are quotations in the book, that is how the chord or phrase would be spoken if someone was telling how the song goes. You will be able to discuss number charts and talk chord progressions with other musicians. If somebody yells, **"Fifteen Eleven"** across a stage, you'll know it's the chords for 4 bars of the song and not a football score. "Fifteen Eleven", said so simply contains enough information to get you through the entire intro to a song you've never heard. In addition, this book teaches terms used to describe feel and style for different types of music. It's important to know musician terminology. Otherwise it can be really frustrating trying to describe what you're hearing in your head.

•Included with NNS 7 is a cd of instrumentals, called *String Of Pearls*. I wrote all but one of the songs to demonstrate different feels, how to understand counting bars and feel phrases. For example, *Winter Break* is an 8ths Country Rock, *Waylon* is **6/8** with a Halftime feel and *Pelican Shuffle* is a 2 beat shuffle that goes into a Ray Price style shuffle during the choruses.

•Each of the 10 songs has 5 charts handwritten by some of Nashville's best known musicians: **Charlie McCoy, David Briggs, Lura Foster, Jimmy Capps, Brent Rowan, John Hobbs, Biff Watson, Tony Harrell, Chris Farren, Mike Chapman and Eddie Bayers.** For example, the song *String Of Pearls* has charts written by: **Charlie McCoy, Brent Rowan, John Hobbs, Jimmy Capps and Biff Watson**. The song, *Waylon* has charts written by: **Jimmy Capps, Biff Watson, Tony Harrell, Lura Foster, and Eddie Bayers**.

As you listen to the cd, you'll be able to compare some of the different styles of notation and symbols these musicians use to chart the same piece of music. The different charts show the kinds of numbering techniques that you are liable to run into in almost all of the major recording and television studios, clubs, showcases, rehearsal halls, and other situations where music is performed in Nashville.

•In NNS edition 7, I rewrote all the book's number system examples and figures by hand. When there are theory and traditional notational figures, I left as print, because I don't write notation as well as this computer. The Nashville Number System is still best written by hand, in my opinion. Anyway, this whole book is about handwritten number charts.

•*String Of Pearls* is also an **extended cd**. As well as high quality audio that will play in your cd player, you can insert the disk into your computer and watch animated number charts as you listen to the songs. There is a click track with each song and a highlight that moves in time with each chord change. You can see exactly how to count each measure, even though each song has a different feel. Counting bars is probably the hardest part of the number system to teach. As a result, you will be able to *see, hear and feel* how these charts work.

•Another new addition to this book is a collection of charts handwritten by some of Nashville's best musicians and producers. 17 people who are doing sessions everyday and really influencing how music is made in Nashville, were kind enough to send me session charts they had written. Some of these players, like Dann Huff, you may have heard of from producing Keith Urban and LeAnn Rimes, but you may not have heard of Jeff King, who's played guitar on records by Reba McIntyre, Phil Vassar and Randy Travis; or Mike Chapman, who played bass on all of Garth Brooks records. Search these musicians on www.allmusic.com and see your favorite records that these musicians have played on.

So, whether you are a songwriter trying to get your material performed, a band leader teaching songs from a record, a producer teaching an arrangement or a musician learning an arrangement in the studio, the *Nashville Number System* is a great way of presenting your songs and musical ideas.

Major Scales and Number Substitution Table

Key	⸢Whole Step⸣		⸢Whole Step⸣		⸢Half Step⸣	⸢Whole Step⸣		⸢Whole Step⸣		⸢Whole Step⸣		⸢Half Step⸣
1	♯1 or ♭2	2	♯2 or ♭3	3	4	♯4 or ♭5	5	♯5 or ♭6	6	♯6 or ♭7	7	1
A	A♯ or B♭	B	B♯ or C	C♯	D	D♯ or E♭	E	E♯ or F	F♯	F♯♯ or G	G♯	A
A♯	A♯♯ or B	B♯	B♯♯ or C♯	C♯♯	D♯	D♯♯ or E	E♯	E♯♯ or F♯	F♯♯	F♯♯♯ or G♯	G♯♯	A♯
B♭	B or C♭	C	C♯ or D♭	D	E♭	E or F♭	F	F♯ or G♭	G	G♯ or A♭	A	B♭
B	B♯ or C	C♯	C♯♯ or D	D♯	E	E♯ or F	F♯	F♯♯ or G	G♯	G♯♯ or A	A♯	B
C	C♯ or D♭	D	D♯ or E♭	E	F	F♯ or G♭	G	G♯ or A♭	A	A♯ or B♭	B	C
C♯	C♯♯ or D	D♯	D♯♯ or E	E♯	F♯	F♯♯ or G	G♯	G♯♯ or A	A♯	A♯♯ or B	B♯	C♯
D♭	D or E♭♭	E♭	E or F♭	F	G♭	G or A♭♭	A♭	A or B♭♭	B♭	B or C♭	C	D♭
D	D♯ or E♭	E	E♯ or F	F♯	G	G♯ or A♭	A	A♯ or B♭	B	B♯ or C	C♯	D
D♯	D♯♯ or E	E♯	E♯♯ or F♯	F♯♯	G♯	G♯♯ or A	A♯	A♯♯ or B	B♯	B♯♯ or C♯	C♯♯	D♯
E♭	E or F♭	F	F♯ or G♭	G	A♭	A or B♭♭	B♭	B or C♭	C	C♯ or D♭	D	E♭
E	E♯ or F	F♯	F♯♯ or G	G♯	A	A♯ or B♭	B	B♯ or C	C♯	C♯♯ or D	D♯	E
F	F♯ or G♭	G	G♯ or A♭	A	B♭	B or C♭	C	C♯ or D♭	D	D♯ or E♭	E	F
F♯	F♯♯ or G	G♯	G♯♯ or A	A♯	B	B♯ or C	C♯	C♯♯ or D	D♯	D♯♯ or E	E♯	F♯
G♭	G or A♭♭	A♭	A or B♭♭	B♭	C♭	C or D♭♭	D♭	D or E♭♭	E♭	E or F♭	F	G♭
G	G♯ or A♭	A	A♯ or B♭	B	C	C♯ or D♭	D	D♯ or E♭	E	E♯ or F	F♯	G
G♯	G♯♯ or A	A♯	A♯♯ or B	B♯	C♯	C♯♯ or D	D♯	D♯♯ or E	E♯	E♯♯ or F♯	F♯♯	G♯
A♭	A or B♭♭	B♭	B or C♭	C	D♭	D or E♭♭	E♭	E or F♭	F	F♯ or G♭	G	A♭

Using the Major Scale and Number Substitution Table

Use the Major Scale Number Substitution Table on page 4 to determine what number your chord is, or the chord for which you have a number. The Step Formula for finding the major scale is at the top of the chart. Each major scale is spelled from the left to right with large letters. Chromatic half steps between each whole step degree of the scale are in small letters.

Use this table the same way you would use the table in a road atlas to find the distance between two cities. Find your key in the far left column. Search the horizontal row of the key you are in for the chord whose number you need to find. When you find the chord, from there follow the column upward to discover the corresponding number.

Likewise, if you need to know what chord a certain number is, find the number at the top of the table. Then, follow that column down until you reach the horizontal spelling of the scale for your key. The two columns should intersect at the correct chord.

If you are playing your song on guitar and using a capo, assign numbers to chords as if you're not using a capo at all. For instance, if your song is in the key of **D**, but you're capoed to the second fret, you will be playing with chord forms as if you're in the key of **C**. So you may read the table as if you are in the key of **C** instead of **D**. The numbers will be the same for both keys.

One more thing, though we know that **B♯** and **C** are the same note, correct alphabetical spelling of the A major scale dictates that the ♯2 must be a **B♯**. Since there is no **B♯** in the chromatic scale, for simplicity, in the key of **A**, call **C** the ♭3. Adhering to the same spelling rule, the ♯6 in **A** should be **F♯♯** (F double sharp). **F♯♯** is the same note as **G**, so we'll use **G** as the ♭7 in the key of **A**, instead of **F♯♯** as the ♯6.

The Major Scale Derivation

Chromatic Scale

The chromatic scale is composed of all 12 notes within an octave, beginning with and including the tonic, or *1*, for which the scale is named. To play an **A** chromatic scale on guitar, start with the open fifth string, **A**, and play the note on every fret upward until you reach the next **A** note on the 12th fret, one octave above.

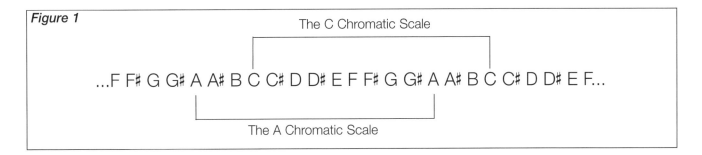

Intervals

An interval is the distance between two notes. **A** to **A♯** (A Sharp) is a half step, or minor 2nd interval. **A** to **B** is a whole step, or major 2nd interval. Two half steps equal a whole step, regardless of the spelling. For instance, there is no note between **E** and **F**, so **E** to **F** is only a half step, while **E** to **F♯** is a whole step. The same holds true for the interval between **B** and **C**. There is no other note between **B** and **C**, so **B** to **C** represents a half step. **C** to **C♯** also represents a half step, so a whole step up from **B** is **C♯**. One half step down from **B** is **B♭** (B flat). Whenever notes or chords move up or down in a series of half steps, it is called, moving "chromatically."

Step Formula

The step formula is a way of extracting a major scale from the chromatic scale. It tells which intervals to use to determine each degree of the major scale. The step formula remains constant, so a major scale can be found, beginning with the tonic, or *1* of any key.

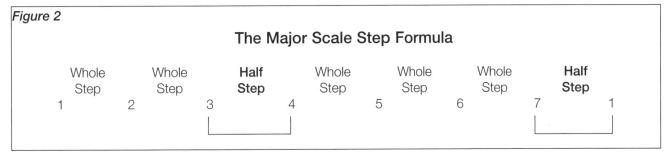

The Major Scale and Number Substitution

The major scale consists of seven notes, which are derived alphabetically from the chromatic scale by applying the step formula. Flip back to page 9 and refer to the Step Formula in Figure 2 as you read the following paragraphs.

To spell a major scale, begin with the "tonic," or *1*, for which the scale is named. This will become the name of the key we are working in. You can spell a major scale in any key, although for our example, we will show you how to spell the **A** major scale. Therefore, **A** is the tonic, or *1*.

Applying the step formula, we find that the second note or degree of the scale must be a whole step up from the *1*. Spelling alphabetically up the chromatic scale one whole step, we see that **B** is the second degree, or *2* of the **A** major scale.

To find the third degree of the **A** major scale, spell ahead a whole step from the *2*. **B** to **C** is only a half step, so a whole step from **B** is **C♯**. Therefore, **C♯** is the third degree, or *3* of the **A** major scale. A question arises, though... isn't **C♯** the same note as **D♭**? Well, yes, it sounds the same, but remember, we're spelling *alphabetically*, so the whole step up from **B** is spelled **C♯** instead of **D♭**.

We look again at the step formula to determine that the interval between the third and fourth notes of the scale needs to be a half step. So, we spell ahead one half step from **C♯**, the *3*, to **D**, which will be the fourth degree, or *4*, in the key of **A**.

Next, according to the step formula, we must spell ahead one whole step from **D**, the *4*, to determine the *5* note of the A major scale. Therefore, **E** is the *5*.

Likewise, the *6* is a whole step from the *5*. **E** to **F** is only one half step, so a whole step from **E** is **F♯**. **F♯** is the *6*.

One alphabetical whole step farther, we find that **G♯** is the seventh degree, or *7* of the A major scale.

Finally, according to the step formula, from the *7*, spell ahead one half step to reach the *1* again, which will be one octave above the **A** note where we began.

So, by spelling alphabetically up the chromatic scale, beginning with the tonic of the key you are in, and using intervals which are predetermined by the step formula, we've written the **A** major scale.

Pick any note and you can sing its major scale with "Do Re Mi". Play any note on the guitar or piano and sing Do, Re, Mi from there. That will be your major scale for that key. Do is *1*, Re is *2*, Mi is *3*, and so forth, until you reach Do, or *1*, one octave higher, no matter which note you start from.

Figure 3

Do	Re	Mi	Fa	So	La	Ti	Do
1	2	3	4	5	6	7	1

The step formula remains constant, regardless of which key you're spelling. In every major scale, there will be a half step between *Mi* and *Fa* and a half step between the *Ti* and *Do*. There will be a whole step interval between all the other degrees of the major scale.

The Nashville Numbers

In the Nashville system, numbers assigned to each step of the major scale represent chords as well as single notes. In the key of **A**, we have the major scale **A B C♯ D E F♯ G♯**. This major scale become chords *1 2 3 4 5 6 7*. **A** is the *1* chord and **G♯** is the 7 chord. You've probably heard of a " **I, IV, V** " blues progression. It's the same in Nashville. In the key of **A**: **I, IV** and **V** is **A**, **D** and **E**, but it's written with numbers *1*, *4* and *5* instead of Roman Numerals. This may seem too simple, but the Nashville numbers are assigned directly to the major scale for the key that your song is in. It gets better.

Still in the key of **A**, what if our song goes to a **G** chord instead of a **G♯** chord? If we flat or lower the **G♯**, or 7 chord, one half step we have the **G**, or ♭*7* chord, we need for our song.

In the key of **A**, how do we determine what number to assign a **C** chord? Well, we know that **C♯** is the *3* chord, and **C** is one half step below **C♯**. So, one half step below the *3* chord is the ♭*3* or "flat three" chord.

Likewise, what is the ♭*6* chord in the key of **A**? Simply determine the *6* chord and flat it one half step. **F♯** is the *6*, therefore **F** is the ♭*6* chord.

On the other hand, to find the ♯*4* or "sharp four" chord, determine the *4* chord and raise or sharp it one half step. In the key of **A**, **D** is the **4 chord**, therefore **D♯** is the ♯*4* or "sharp four" chord.

A lot of musicians like to place the sharp or flat sign after the chord number. For example: *7*♭, *3*♭ or *4*♯ would be called *"seven flat, three flat or four sharp"*. This is because the number is substituted for the chord's proper name. You would say "E♭" not "♭E."

The other way is to think of a number is not only as a chord's proper name, but also as its *function* within a progression. When analyzing traditional jazz harmony, you use Roman numerals to identify a chord's function in any key. A substitute chord like a ♭II⁷ has the flat sign in front of the chord to show how the chord was altered from the major scale. In which case, you have: ♭*7*, ♭*3* or ♯*4*; said,*"flat seven, flat three or sharp four"*.

The **I** chord is the tonic and is built on the first note of its major scale. It establishes the key and is usually the final resting point for the progression. The **V**⁷ chord is called the dominant. It carries tension and makes you want to resolve back to the **I**. These are chord functions. All chords function to move a progression forward ultimately to a final rest at the **I** chord.

In Nashville, we use numbers instead of Roman numerals. The numbers still dictate function within a progression and the flat or sharp sign before a number shows what you did to that chord with relationship to the major scale.

Another question: Why write a ♯*4* chord instead of a ♭*5* chord since they are the same? Likewise, why a ♭*7* instead of a ♯*6* ? Most of the time you use flatted chords ♭*2*, ♭*3*, ♭*5*, ♭*6* and ♭*7*. However, in a progression that is moving up in half steps or "chromatically", a passing chord would be written as a sharp. For a progression moving chromatically downward, the passing chord would be a flat. For example, when moving chromatically from the *1* to the *2*, you write *1* ♯*1* *2*. On the other hand, in the case of the *2* down to the *1*, you write *2* ♭*2* *1*.

Relative Minor

The *6* note of any major scale is the *1*, or tonic, of that scale's relative minor key. For example, in the key **C**, the *6* is **A**. Therefore **A** minor is the relative minor of the key of **C** major. The same notes are used for each scale, except that the **A** relative minor scale begins with **A** and the half steps fall between the *2* and *3*, and the *5* and *6*.

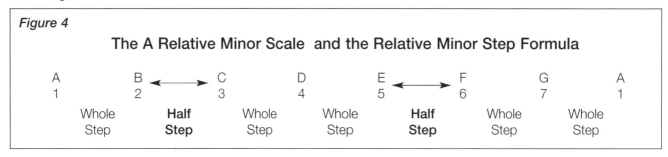

Take, for instance, *The House of the Rising Sun*, in **A minor**. **A minor** is the tonic or *1* **minor chord**.

Figure 5

E Relative Minor Scale

E	F#	G	A	B	C	D	E
1	2	3	4	5	6	7	1

Half Step (between 2 and 3), Half Step (between 5 and 6)

Study Figure 5 for a moment to see how the relative minor step formula is used to construct the E relative minor scale. Notice that this **E minor** scale uses the same notes as the **G major** scale. Both the **G major** scale and the **E minor** scale have an F#.

Having said all that... In Nashville, *most of the time*, for a song in a minor key, chord charts are written as if in the relative major key. Even if **A minor** sounds like the actual tonic, or *1* **minor** chord, the chart is written as if in the key of **C major**. In which case the **A minor** chord is written as the **6 minor**. The majority of popular songs that sound as if in a minor key, often resolve to the relative major anyway. It is therefore, important to know how to find the relative major of a minor key. Here's how to do it.

If your song sounds like it's in a minor key, but you want to chart it in the relative major key, first determine the tonic minor chord. Then to find the relative major of that minor key, spell upward from the tonic note for which the minor scale is named, 3 half steps. That note will be the relative major key. On the previous page, in Figure 4 (which uses the **A minor** scale) spell upward 3 half steps from the *1* (**A**→ **A#**, **A#** → **B**, **B**→ **C**) to find that **C** is the relative major of the key of **A minor**. If you were writing a chart for *The House of the Rising Sun* (which is in **A minor**) and wanted to write it in the relative major (which is **C major**), then **A minor** is the **6 minor chord**, **C** is the **1 chord**, **D** is the **2 chord**, **F** is the **4 chord** and **E**^{7} is the **3**^{7} **chord**.

Another example is, if you were playing *Ghost Riders In the Sky* in the key of **E minor**. The tonic chord sounds like **E minor**. However, you find the relative major (**G**) and write the chart in the key of **G**. The first chord of the song is **E minor** and will be written as *6-*. The **G** chord in the chorus will be written as *1*.

There are times, however, that I would chart a song using the minor key. It would usually be a song with very simple chord changes, like "The Thrill Is Gone", by B.B.King. This song, charted in minor would have the chords: *1 minor*, *4 minor*, *5⁷* and *♯5*. If you used the relative major to chart "The Thrill...", the chords would be: *6 minor*, *2 minor*, *4* and *3⁷*. It's weird to be looking at a *3⁷ chord*, but hearing the *5⁷ chord*, and feel all the functions associated with the *5⁷*; wanting to resolve to the *1 chord*. It really depends on what you're comfortable with and who you're writing a chart for. If the song has some complicated chords and resolves to the relative major for the Chorus or Bridge, I'd probably write the chart using the relative major key and have the *6 minor* work as the tonic instead of *1 minor*.

Chord Symbols

In addition to assigning each chord a number, we must designate whether the chord is a major or minor, and if it carries a seventh, a major seventh, etc.

A major chord needs no symbol. The number by itself always means that it is a basic major chord. Minor chords carry a minus sign to the right of the chord number, *6-* . You may also use a small *m* for minor, but that can sometimes be confused with major.

Chord voicing (ninths, sixths, sevenths, etc.) appear as smaller numbers to the upper right of the chord, *5⁷*.

Some chords are played with a different bass note, for example, a *4* chord with a *5* note in the bass. This is written as a fraction, $\frac{4}{5}$, and called a "four over five." For example, progressions with the moving bass lines like the first four measures of Mr. Bojangles can be written as shown below in Figure 6.

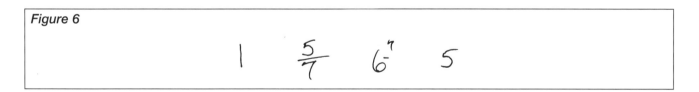

Figure 6

Another common walk down is *4* down to *1*. Figure 7.

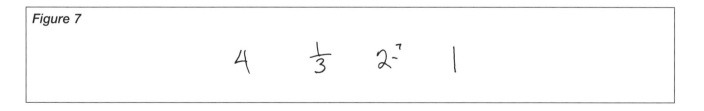

Figure 7

Figure 8   # Chord Symbol Chart

Major	1		
Major Seventh	1△	1maj 7	
Major Ninth	1△9	1maj 9	
Dominant Seventh	1^7		
Sixth	1^6		
Ninth	1^9		
Major add 9	1$^{add\ 9}$		
Minor	6-	6^m	6^{min}
Minor Seventh	6-^{7}	6^{m7}	6$^{min\ 7}$
Minor Sixth	6-^{6}	6^{m6}	6$^{min\ 6}$
Minor Major Seventh	6-△	6^{m}△	6-$^{maj\ 7}$
Augmented	5$^+$		
Augmented Seventh	5^{+7}		
Diminished	#4°		
Diminished Seventh	#4$^{\circ 7}$		
Minor Seven Flat Five or Half Diminished	7-$^{7\ b5}$	7$^\varnothing$	
Seven with a flat 9	5$^{7\ b9}$		
Eleven	5^{11}		
Thirteen	5^{13}		

Time

Time Signatures

A time signature must be denoted before a chart is begun. The time signature tells how many beats may fit in one measure as well as the time value of each beat.

Take, for example, a time signature of 4/4 (read as "four, four"). The top number dictates that four beats will be counted in each measure. The bottom number specifies that each of the 4 beats will be counted with a quarter note value. In other words, one measure of 4/4 will contain a total of four quarter note beats. Time signatures, however, do not indicate the tempo (speed) at which the beats will be counted and played.

Common Time Signatures

4/4 4 beats per measure, a quarter note gets one beat (ex.: *On the Other Hand*, by Randy Travis)

2/4 2 beats per measure, a quarter note gets one beat (ex.: *Rocky Top*, by The Osborne Brothers)

3/4 3 beats per measure, a quarter note gets one beat (ex.: *Rose Colored Glasses*, by John Conlee)

6/8 6 beats per measure, an eighth note gets one beat (ex.: *Mammas, Don't Let Your Babies Grow Up to Be Cowboys*, by Waylon Jennings)

Although a time signature establishes the number of basic beats a measure will receive, a measure may be subdivided into as many rhythmic variations as called for by the song. However, the totalled rhythmic values of the notes in a measure may not exceed or be less than the total value designated by the time signature.

Note Values

One whole note (o) equals two half notes (♩); one half note (♩) equals two quarter notes (♩); one quarter note (♩) equals two eighth notes (♪); and one eighth note (♪) equals two sixteenth notes (♪). Figure 9 below illustrates the relationship between these five basic note shapes (which represent five basic time values). Each note value is grouped for one complete measure of time.

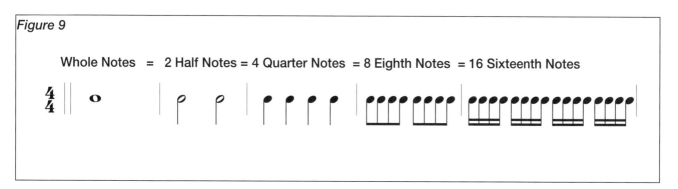

Figure 9

Whole Notes = 2 Half Notes = 4 Quarter Notes = 8 Eighth Notes = 16 Sixteenth Notes

When counting a measure of **4/4**, you count "1, 2, 3, 4." If you are counting eighth notes, you count "1 and, 2 and, 3 and, 4 and." Each number is an eighth note down-beat, while the "and" stands for an eighth note upbeat.

So, one beat of **4/4** gets "1 and," or 2 eighth notes. If you are counting sixteenth notes, count a measure of **4/4** as shown below in Figure 10.

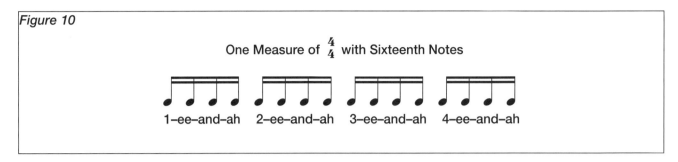

In each of the examples that follow in Figure 11 the measures are subdivided differently, but they all have the total number of time as dictated by the time signature.

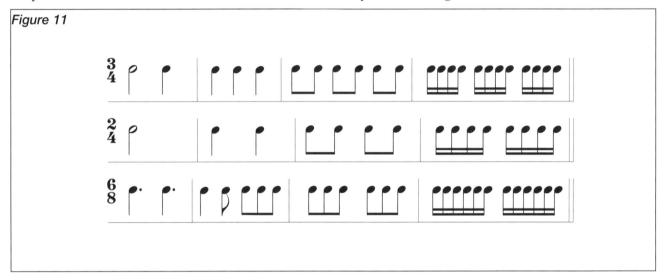

Rests

When there is no musical activity going on within a measure, time must still be counted and notated with the proper value of rest.

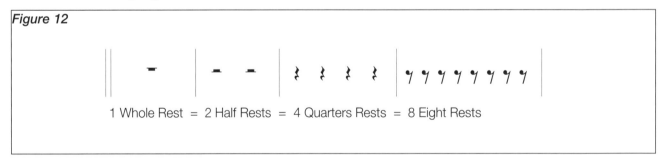

In formal music, whole note rests and half note rests are drawn on separate staff lines. Since there are no staff lines in the Nashville system, we use only a portion of the staff line to differentiate whole note rests from half note rests (Figure 12). Also, be careful to keep quarter note rests from looking like 3's and eighth note rests from looking like 7's.

Dotted Note

A dot after a note or rest increases the time value of that note by one half of the note dotted.

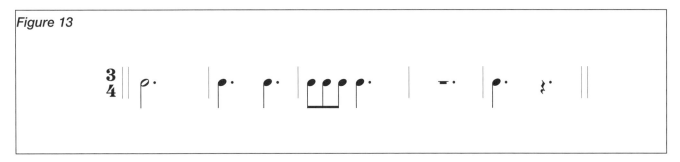
Figure 13

Triplets

An eighth note triplet equals one quarter note. There would be 4 eighth note triplets in a measure of **4/4**.

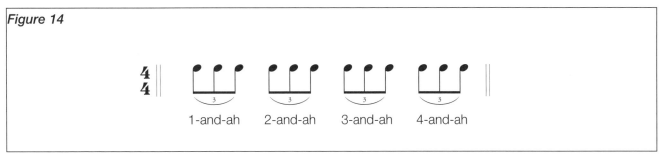
Figure 14

Blueberry Hill and *Unchained Melody* are counted with a slower **2/4** but have a fast triplet or **12/8** feel. If not all the notes of a triplet figure are struck, use an eighth rest in the triplet figure.

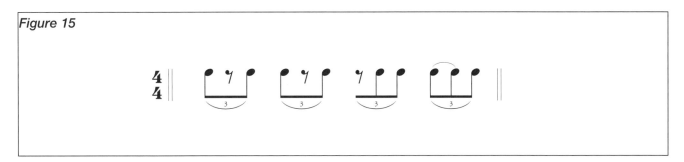
Figure 15

Quarter Note Triplet

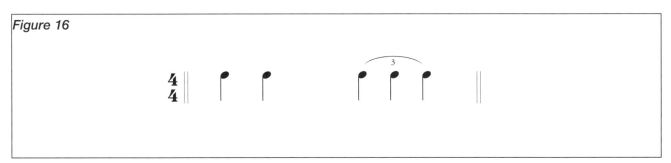
Figure 16

A quarter note triplet equals two beats and has a syncopated feel. In figure 16, the left side of the measure is the same duration as the right side.

Tied Notes

A tied note is struck once and held for the duration of both notes together.

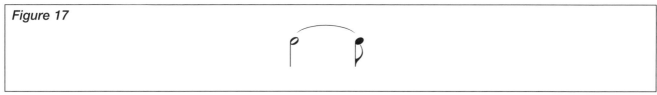
Figure 17

In Figure 17, the note is struck once and held for 2 1/2 beats. If the two notes are a different pitch, the first note is bent smoothly to the second. The second note is not restruck.

Split Bars

In Figure 18a, like in traditional notation, there is one bar, or measure between each bar line.

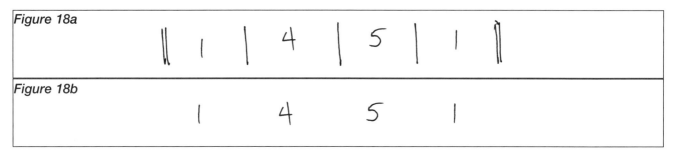
Figure 18a

Figure 18b

However, in the *Nashville Number System*, when a chord number automatically lasts one measure. The divider lines for each measure are not needed. Besides, bar lines are easily confused with the number **1**. Usually there are four measures per line. In Nashville, the line in Figure 18a would be written, instead, as in Figure 18b.

In Figure 19, measures can be subdivided like so:

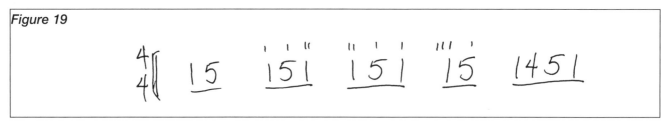
Figure 19

...Or into whatever combinations may fit your song. When more than one chord is written within a measure, the chord numbers are underlined. These measures are called **split bars**. When there is an uneven number of beats per chord, small hash marks over the chord show how many beats each chord gets. When there are two chords in a measure and each gets 2 beats, no hash marks are necessary. The same applies if there are 4 separate chords in a measure of **2/4** . They automatically get one beat each and no hash marks are needed. If a split bar has a syncopated rhythm, or attacks that aren't on the basic downbeat, you may enclose the measure in a box and write the rhythmic phrase in notation above the chord changes.

Some people like to use parentheses around a split bar or divide the measure with a diagonal slash. The slash, however, can make a split bar look like a chord with a different bass note. I like to underline evenly split bars and put more rhythmically complex bars in a box.

Figure 20

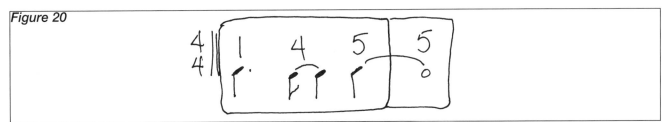

When you use rhythmic notation, you may box in your split bars. In Figure 20, the **4 chord** is pushed or anticipated. It is struck on the "and" of beat 2. Then, the last beat in the first bar is tied to the next measure. The symbol > is an abbreviation for the push, or anticipation, and goes over the chord being pushed. So, another way to write the above example could be Fig. 21.

Figure 21

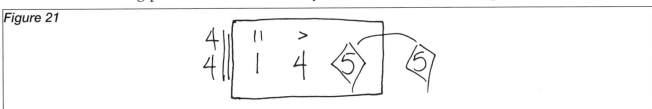

The diamond in Figure 21 is the sign for strike and hold for the designated duration. We'll talk more about diamonds in the section on dynamics. Meanwhile, hash marks over the 1 chord show that it gets 2 beats. It's not necessary to put marks over the other chords because after the push, the measure is divided evenly.

Here are some more rhythmic examples:

Figure 22

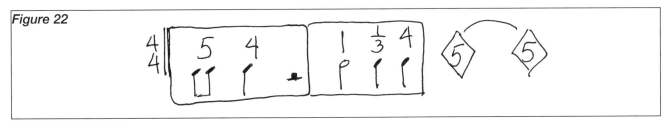

In Figure 22, the **5 chord** is struck with two eighth notes and the **4 chord** gets a quarter note. The remaining 2 beats of the measure get a half note rest. Next bar, the **1 chord** gets a half note, the **1 over 3** and **4 chord** get a quarter note each and the there are 2 measures of **5 diamond** tied together.

New Time Signature

In formal notation, you may change the time signature by writing the new signature in parentheses before the measure that changes; then resume by inserting the original time signature in parentheses in front of it's next measure.

A lot of songs will have a phrase that contains an extra half measure (Figure 23, bar 3).

Figure 23

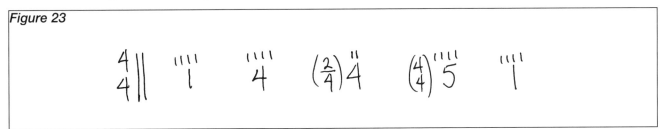

The time signature can change, to allow a song's phrasing to go for an extra half measure before changing back to the original signature. In this case, it's easy to put a **2/4** bar in a box with two hash marks above the number, like in Figure 24a. Figure 24a contains the same line as Figure 23. The boxed measures are **2/4** and get only 2 beats, then **4/4** time automatically resumes without having to re-enter another time signature.

The chord changes from Figure 23 could also be written as in Figure 24a or 24b:

Figure 24a Phrased correctly	4/4‖	1	4	[4]	5	1
Figure 24b Not phrased correctly	4/4‖	1	4	4 5	5 1	[1]

The difference between Figures 24a and 24b is the phrasing. A musical or vocal phrase should start at the beginning of a new measure. In Figure 24b, <u>if the 4 chord in the first half of the third measure is the end of a phrase, and the 5 chord in the second half of the same measure is the beginning of a new phrase</u>, write your chart as in Figure 24a.

A good example of a time signature change and an extra measure is in the intro of *Waylon*, from the cd, *String Of Pearls*. The **2 minor chord** in bar 3 is the end of the musical phrase started in bar 1. Even though the **b3 chord** (bar 4) could technically be a split bar with the **2 minor chord** in bar 3, it is really it's own entity. So, the **2 minor** is best written as a bar of **3/8**, allowing the **b3 chord** to be counted at the beginning of a measure. It's also a lot easier to count the long **b3 diamond** when you look at it as it's own phrase. The **b3 chord** is tied to an extra half measure, so the diamond lasts for a total of 9 beats.

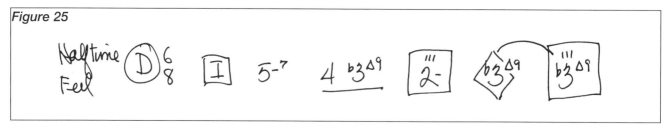

Figure 25

A good example of a song with an extra half measure is, "Mammas Don't Let Your Babies Grow Up To Be Cowboys", by Waylon Jennings. The second line of the chorus has an extra bar of **3/8** to accommodate the lyric,"**lawyers and...**". So, the 2nd line of the chorus would be written as in figure *26a*. Figure *26b* shows improper phrasing with the **1 chord** split in half. You also want to make sure the **1 chord** is the 5th bar of the phrase and at the end of the line, instead of the 1st bar of the next line.

Figure 26a	6/8‖	5	5	5	[5]	1
Figure 26b	6/8‖	5	5	5	5 1	[1]

Melody Notation

The number system can apply to single notes, as well as chords. Numbers are assigned to different notes in a scale the same way they are assigned to different chords. Rhythmic notation is written beneath the number to show the time value of each note. An arrow ↑ or ↓ can show which direction an interval moves from the previous note.

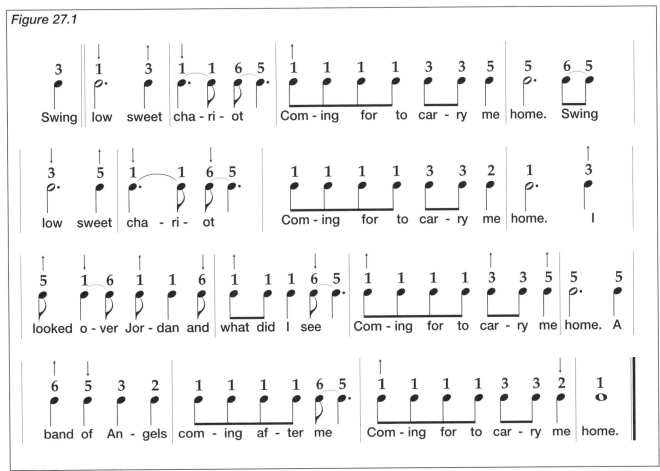

Figure 27.1

Look at Lura Foster's melody notation of String Of Pearls in Fig.27.2. In measure 6 of the verse, notice the arrow showing the 1 note going down to the 3 note instead of up.

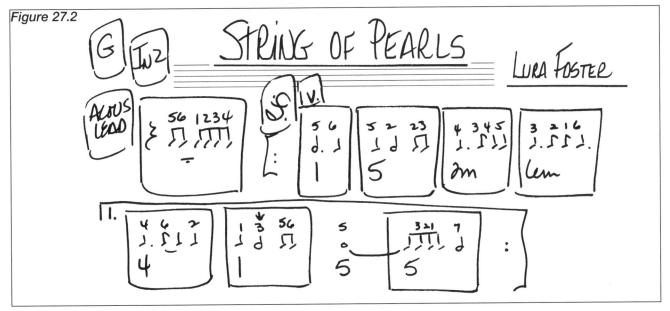

Figure 27.2

━━ Presentation ━━

Structure

It is important that your chart be presented so the organization and arrangement of the song is obvious. A song cannot be played effectively if the musician has to spend more effort reading than playing. Chord changes may go fast, and if a player has to take his eyes off a line to search for information, he can get lost very quickly.

There are usually four measures per line, except where phrasing dictates an extra measure. Measures should line up vertically as well as horizontally. Also, enough space should be allowed between measures so that two measures won't be mistaken for a split bar. A split bar should be able to fit in a line and still allow the next measure to align vertically with the above line. So, as you start a chart, leave yourself room for split bars.

With a fast tempo song, you may run out of room writing 4 bars across the page. In which case, you may start a new column on the other side of the page. Some people prefer to write all the way across the page in groups of four measures. The 8 bars across format can be good with an up tempo song that will have a lot of bars. If you do so, be sure your musicians know that they are reading horizontally.

Figure 28

[I] .... Intro		[TA] .... Turnaround	
[V] .... Verse		[SOLO] .... Instrumental Solo	
[Chnl] .... Channel		[TAG] .... Tag Ending	
[C] .... Chorus			
[B] .... Bridge			

Symbols such as in Figure 28 should label the beginning of each section, and a line should be drawn under each section to separate it from the next section. Separating sections really helps a player keep his place, and is helpful when discussing sections in a song's arrangement.

[I] : **Intro**

The intro is often a short 4 or 8 bar instrumental statement of the melodic hook, or a vamp to establish the groove and set up the mood of the song.

[V] : **Verse**

The verse is the section that describes consequences or tells the story line of a song. There are usually 2 or 3 different verses in a 3 minute song

[Chnl] : **Channel**

The channel is sort of a pre-chorus. It's usually the same section of music each time that builds a transition up to the chorus.

C : **Chorus**

The chorus is the section that delivers the musical hook and is usually the basis for the song. The chorus is often repeated after each verse, and a couple of times at the end to reinforce the hook.

TA : **Turnaround**

A turnaround is a short 4 or 8 bar instrumental restatement of the melodic hook. Often, an instrumental version of the last line or two of the chorus will serve as the turnaround.

B : **Bridge**

This is sometimes called the 'middle 8' (if it's 8 bars), and is usually an 8 to 16 bar interlude that will build to the final chorus.

SOLO : **Solo**

A solo is an instrumental section usually over the chords of a verse or a chorus. If you have a certain instrument in mind, write it by the beginning of the SOLO section. Example: *Guitar/Steel* SOLO : Here the guitar takes the first half of the solo, and the steel plays the second half.

TAG : **Tag**

A tag is usually the last line or two of the final chorus, repeated to signal the end of the song. It sort of puts a cap on the song and is often a repeat of the hook. Be sure to label if a tag is instrumental instead of vocal.

Description

In the upper left hand corner of the chart, write the key, the time signature, the approximate tempo, and a brief description of the feel of the song (Figure 29). A metronome marking for exact tempo can really help a drummer and band dial in the feel you're after.

There should also be any extra information, if necessary, regarding the feel of the song. For example, specific instructions to the bass player like, "Walk the bass.", or for the drummer to play "Rim clicks during the verse and full snare during the chorus." Often, an example of a standard song with a feel similar to yours may really help pinpoint the idea you are going for. Most session charts don't need all this much description because musicians are getting the feel and groove from a demo or the songwriter. However, if you're sitting in or auditioning with a band who's never heard your song, descriptions like this can really narrow down the feel you want.

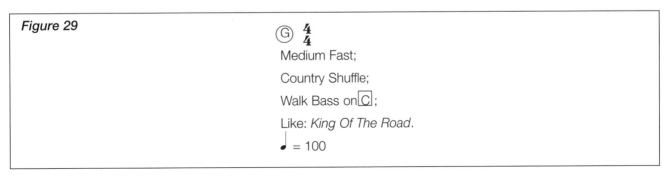

Figure 29

Arranging

Arranging is a good way to create dynamic excitement in your song's performance. For instance, in the margin, you may assign fills and solos to certain instruments, depending on the band's instrumentation and feel you are trying to capture. When you assign an instrument to "fill" a certain verse or chorus, the instrumentalist will play lines that musically fill spaces between lyrics. For example, you may want to assign the fiddle to split the intro with the steel. Then assign the guitar to fill the verse and steel to fill the chorus; then fiddle plays the turn-around.

You may wish to create dynamics by having the whole band layout, except voice and one other instrument. So, you could instruct, "Band out, solo piano and voice." Then, write, "Band enter" at the point you want them continue playing. *"A cappella"*, on the other hand means all music stops, leaving only voices.

If you write no instructions concerning arrangement, the band will usually add dynamics where they feel. Creative freedom given to your musicians, can lead to some nice arranging that may not have been obvious to you before. Many Nashville musicians prefer a "skeleton" number chart with no information other than the numbers to show chord changes. A "skeleton" chart allows a player freedom to add his own arrangement notes and special instructions for his instrument. Of course if you choose to arrange, there will be no question as to where the musicians will fill and solo. This is where you can eliminate questions and decisions, and save rehearsal or studio time. Check out the arrangement below.

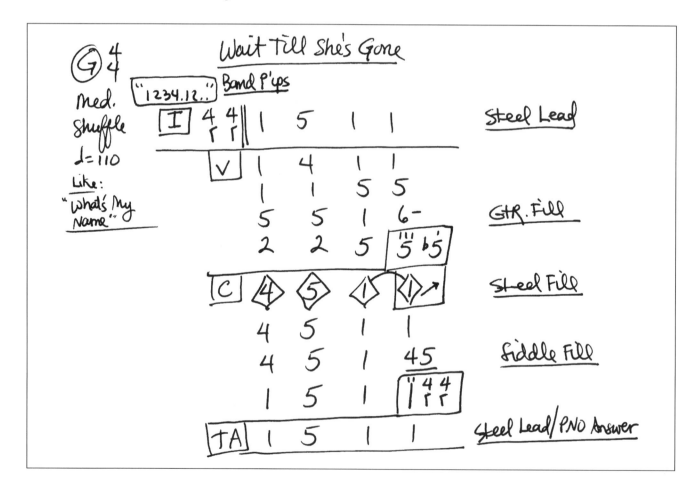

━━ Special Instructions ━━

Tempo

If possible, the exact tempo of a song should be designated with a metronome setting. For example, "♩= 120", means that 4 clicks of a metronome set at 120 will equal one bar of music; also called 120 beats per minute. A musician unfamiliar with a song, and looking at a chart for the first time, may not know whether to read bars with a long, slow count, or *twice* as quickly with a fast count. A song with a halftime feel could be read either way. However, if the player is counting with the wrong tempo, the bars on his chart will be going by either twice as fast or twice as slow as the music is intended. A metronome marking at the top of your chart will eliminate any questions about how the bars are going to be counted.

Count Off

A count off by the drummer, or leader, sets the exact tempo, and allows for any pickup notes to lead into the first measure. A count off is usually two measures, and is counted at the exact tempo with which the song will be played. The proper count off allows a band to begin playing together and to begin playing at the proper tempo. So, if you are counting off your own song, be sure to find the tempo first, then give a 2 measure count at that tempo.

Jimmy Capps sometimes writes the count off that will be given by the drummer. This can be helpful because everyone will know how much of a count to expect, and where the pickup notes begin.

Pickup Notes

Pickup notes are introductory notes that lead into the down beat of the first measure to be played. The pickups are separated from the first measure by a double line. If your song has three quarter note pickups, the drummer would count "1,2,3,4,1..." and the band, or soloist will begin playing the three pickup notes.

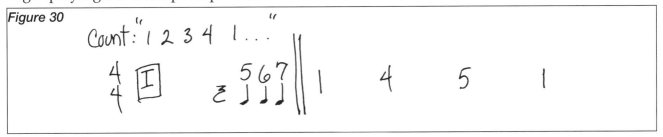

Figure 30

Figure 30 has a two measure count off, and pickups are played on beats "2", "3", & "4" of the second count off measure. Then the first measure of the song begins. Be sure that the pickup notes are not written as part of the first measure. If so, the whole chart will not seem phrased correctly, and may be confusing.

Pickups are usually played by whichever instrument is assigned the lead during the intro. On the other hand, the singer might start the song cold with no instrumental introduction. One example of vocal pickups is *Make The World Go Away*, by Eddy Arnold. Here the vocalist sings for three beats, and the band begins on the second syllable of "away", which is the first down beat of the chorus. So, for the intro of *Make The World Go Away*, write three beats of rest and a memo that there are solo vocal pickups (Figure 31).

Figure 31

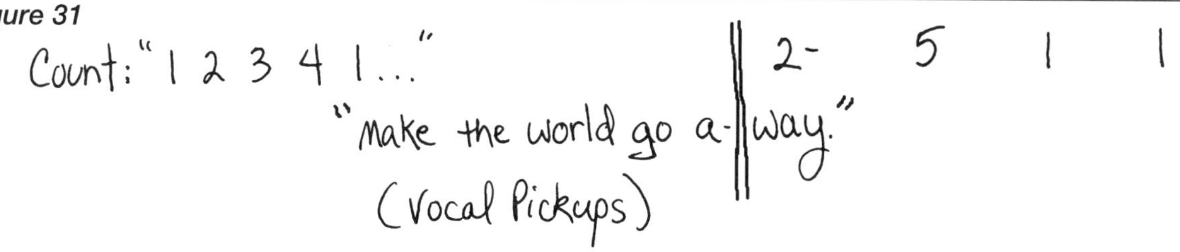

Count: "1 2 3 4 1..."   ‖ 2-   5 | |
"make the world go a-‖way."
(Vocal Pickups)

Extra Measure

An extra measure is sometimes added at the end of the line to provide time for an extended vocal phrase or note, or to make room for an instrumental or vocal pickup to the next phrase. We talked extra measures on page 19, under the section called *New Time Signatures*. An extra measure often provides space for a singer to keep phrasing even. There may be more than one extra measure, but they are written to the right of the measure whose phrase they extend. The important idea is to have the beginning of a musical or vocal phrase start at the beginning of a new line.

The song *Daddy's Hands*, by Holly Dunn counted in cut time, has an extra measure at the end of the 2nd and 3rd lines of the chorus. Figure 32 is the chorus of *Daddy's Hands*. Notice the extra measures at the end of the 2nd and 3rd lines instead of at the beginning of the lines that follow.

Figure 32

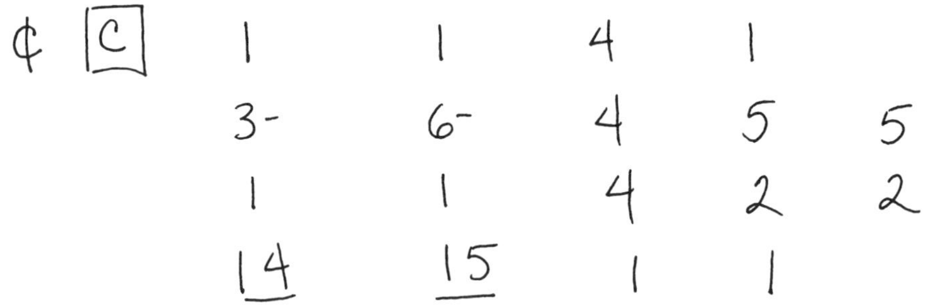

¢ [C] | | 4 |
        3-   6-   4   5   5
        | | 4   2   2
        |4 |5 | |

Repeat Signs ‖: :‖

Play from one repeat sign to the other, return to the first and repeat everything between the signs. Then, move on to the next section.

For example, if a verse is played twice in a row, but has a slightly different ending the second time, you may use repeat signs and write a first and second ending. In Figure 33, play through the 1st ending. Take the repeat and play the section again. The second time, skip the 1st ending, play the 2nd ending and go on to the next section.

Figure 33

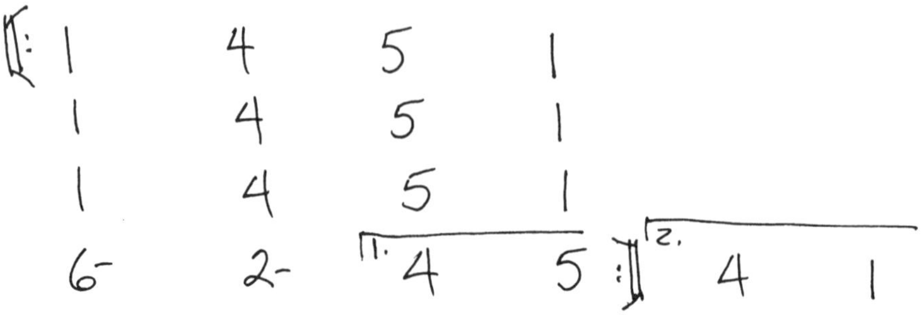

‖: | 4   5 |
    | 4   5 |
    | 4   5 |
    6-   2- |¹· 4   5 :‖ |²· 4 |

If the section included needs repeating more than once for instance, write 3x's by the last repeat sign, like in Figure 34.

Figure 34

V ‖: 1	4	5	1
	1	4	5	1
C 4/4	4/4	1	1 :‖ 3 x's

It's usually best to write out an entire section rather than try to save space by repeating lines within a section. In other words, in a 16 bar Verse, you wouldn't write repeats around the 1st line and instructions to repeat those 4 bars 4x's. Write out the entire verse.

D.S. al ⊕

D.S. is an abbreviation of the latin instruction to return to the sign (𝄋). *Al* ⊕, means play to the Coda (⊕). *D.S. al* ⊕ could be used as a short cut if there is a difference between two sections, so you won't have to write out the whole section again.

Figure 35

I	1	5	1	1
V 𝄋	1	4	5	1
	6-	2-	5	1
C	4	4	1	1 ⊕
	1	5	1	1 D.𝄋. al Coda ⊕
⊕	1	5	5	|5 1‿|

In Figure 35, play the first verse and chorus until it says *D.S. al* ⊕ We return to the sign 𝄋 and play the verse a second time to the coda ⊕. Then, we jump to the other coda ⊕, skipping the last line of the second chorus and instead, playing the Coda line. *D.C. al* ⊕ is the same as *D.S. al* ⊕, except *D.C.* means return to the very beginning of the song, instead of the 𝄋 then play to the coda, ⊕.

Please consider though, that short cuts can be confusing. With a *D.S. al* ⊕, the player has to take his eyes off the chart to find the 𝄋 then again to search for the new ⊕. Sometimes it is safer to write out the entire section rather than save a little ink on a short cut.

Vamp

Sometimes, for an intro, recitation section of a song, or fade, you may want the band to fall into a holding pattern over a certain progression. This is called a vamp. The band vamps over the section which is enclosed with repeat signs until the leader cues to move on to the next section.

Figure 36

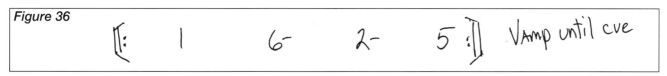

Modulation

A modulation is when you change keys during a song. There are many ways to modulate. One of the more common ways is to go straight to the new key. After the last bar in the original key, write *Mod* ↗, and the amount of steps involved, or the chord of the song to which you're modulating, and encircle the new key. Immediately after the modulation sign, (*Mod* ↗), the chord numbers will not change, but they will be read as in the new key. In Figure 37, the first line ends with a **C** chord, or *1*, in the key of **C**. The first chord which appears after the modulation is now a **D**, or *1* in the key of **D**.

Figure 37

| Key of Ⓒ | 1 | 4 | 5 | 1 | Mod ↗ 1 Step |
| Key of Ⓓ | 1 | 4 | 5 | 1 | |

Another type of modulation is to use the *5* chord of the new key, or the "New 5", and then write modulation instructions. In Figure 38, the *6* is the *5* of the new key, but is written as the *6* in the original key.

Figure 38

| Key of Ⓒ | 1 | 4 | 5 | 6 | Mod ↗ 1 Step |
| Key of Ⓓ | 1 | 4 | 5 | 1 | |

If you wanted to modulate only a half step use #*5* as the new *5*. In Figure 39, #*5* will be the *5* of the new key of **C♯**, a half step above the original key of **C**.

Figure 39

| Key of Ⓒ | 1 | 4 | 5 | #5 | Mod ↗ ½ Step |
| Key of Ⓒ♯ | 1 | 4 | 5 | 1 | |

Look at Figure 40. We're modulating more than a step: C up to E♭. You can say," Mod ↗ to ♭*3*", which is ♭*3* of the old key (C), but becomes *1* of the new key (E♭). Brent Rowan would then write *3*♭ =*1*. So, in Figure 40, the 1st chord after the modulation is *4* in the key of E♭, or an A♭.

Figure 40

| Key of Ⓒ | 1 | 4 | 5 | 1 | Mod ↗ to ♭3 |
| Key of Ⓔ♭ | 4 | 5 | 1 | 1 | |

Walkups and Walkdowns

Sometimes, when you have a basic scalar walkup or walkdown from one chord to the next, you may abbreviate the notation with an arrow pointing in the direction of the target chord.

Figure 41

The above line can be written like in the example below: Figure 42.

Figure 42

Remember though, the arrow is simple shorthand and will work only in place of a quarter note, major scale approach to the new chord. Notice how measure 1 in Figure 41 is a split bar and the *1* chord gets 2 beats. Therefore, the arrow can represent only a 2 beat walkup. As follows, the *5* chord in the third measure gets one beat allowing time for a three beat walkdown.

Speaking Numbers In Nashville

Sometimes at a session, someone will read their chart for the other musicians to copy. Or at a gig, without charts, the leader may need to tell how the song goes. In which case, you talk in phrases of 4 chords when possible. For example, "Fifteen Eleven." would be a bar of **1**, a bar of **5**, and two bars of **1**. That could be the whole intro to a song. "Fifty Five Fifty One." would be three bars of **5** and one bar of **1**. This one's a little more complicated: "Fifteen, Five Split Four, Three Minor Split Two Minor, With One Beat On The Two Minor." would be a bar of **1**, a bar of **5**, an even split bar with the first half a **5 chord** and the second half a **4 chord** and another split bar, but with three beats on the **3 minor chord** and one beat on the **2 minor chord**. You see how a band can communicate quickly with numbers when they need to.

Below is the verse to the song, *Waylon*, from the *String Of Pearls* cd. Here's how you would say it: "Eleven Forty Four. Fifty-Five, Five Split Flat Seven, One, One Diamond Split Flat Three Major Nine."

Waylon Verse

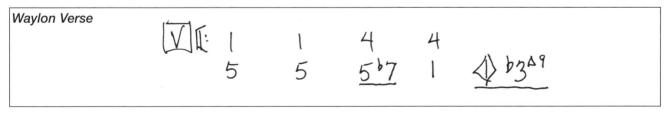

If you hear someone say, "Put a *Batman* on the **1 chord**", that would mean a quarter note with a sharp cut off and a dotted half note sustaining for the last three beats of the bar. We're getting into some real slang here, though.

Dynamics

Dynamics

There are several signs which tell a player how to attack a note, or perhaps how not to attack it. There are signs for loudness, sustain, anticipation, speed, punch, and other ways of playing a note or chord. These different approaches to a certain note or phrase are called dynamics. Dynamic indicators can really help communicate the kind of feeling and personality you want translated into the music.

Diamond ◊

A diamond means to strike the chord and let it ring for its designated duration. Simply draw a diamond around the chord to be held. Below, the final bar, called a *"One diamond"*, is struck and held for one full measure, or 4 beats.

Figure 43

Some people write small diamonds above or below the chord, as in Figure 44.

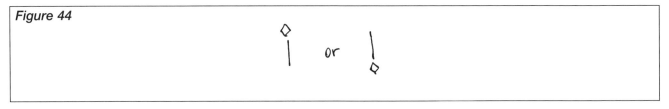
Figure 44

A tied diamond shows that the chord is held for the extra duration notated. In Figure 45, the 5 chord in the third measure is struck and held for its measure plus the next measure, or a total of eight beats.

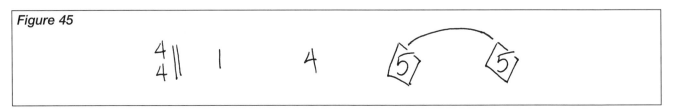
Figure 45

Bird's Eye or Fermata ⌒

The bird's eye is a symbol taken from formal notation. When placed over the chord, it means the chord is struck and held until there is a cue from whoever is conducting the band. For example, in the tag of *Forever and Ever Amen*, by Randy Travis, the band hits the chord and holds it while Randy sings, "Amen." There is no countable way for the band to come back in together, so they must rely on a hand signal, or cue from whoever is conducting the ending. A few Nashville musicians will use a Bird's Eye instead of a Diamond. So, you can't say I didn't warn you.

Cut Off or Mute

A ▲ or • above the chord means that the chord is struck and muted, or cut off. You don't allow the chord to ring for the full beat. Here, the ↑1 is struck and muted, though the full measure is counted.

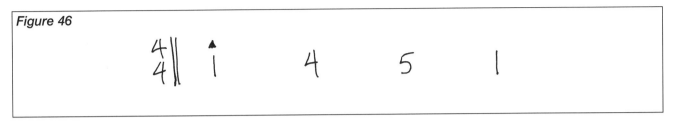
Figure 46

In Figure 47, there is a bar with two muted attacks on the *1* chord plus a 2 beat rest.

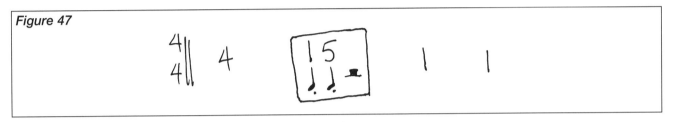
Figure 47

Anticipation >

Below, the *6-* is struck on the "and" or upbeat of beat 2 of the measure.

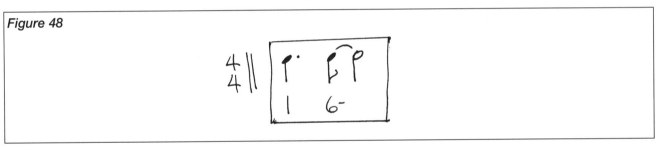
Figure 48

A small horizontal arrow over a chord can also mean that the chord is anticipated or pushed. Figure 49 is a fast, easy way to write Figure 48, using the push sign. It is true, this arrow is a dynamics symbol borrowed from traditional notation.

Figure 49

One thing you'll notice when looking through the charts in this book, are all the different symbols people use for push signs.

Loudness

The loudness sign is written beneath a passage or phrase. When pointing to the right, it means to begin reducing the volume at the open end, and be the quietest at the tip of the sign. On the contrary, when the loudness sign points to the left, it means to begin increasing in volume at the closed point, and be the loudest where the sign is open. These symbols are good for writing in a big crescendo, or setting up a really quiet passage for dynamic contrast.

In Figure 50, begin volume increase at the second measure and be loudest at the fourth measure.

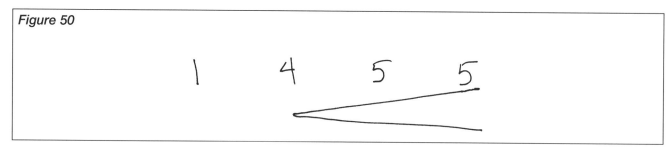

In Figure 51, begin volume decrease at the second measure and be the quietest at the fourth measure.

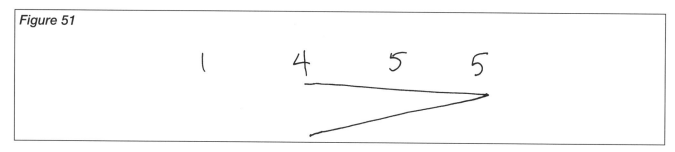

Ritard *rit.*

The ritard sign under a section means to gradually slow down tempo. Begin slowing at the *Ritard* sign and continue slowing until the end of the sign. *Ritards* are effective for dramatically bringing the dynamics down to a quieter level or ending a song. However, if you want to *ritard* during the song and then return to the original tempo, write *"a tempo"* where the original tempo should resume.

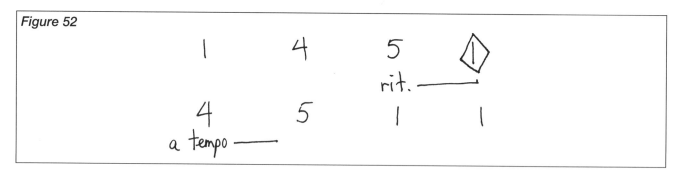

Feel and Style

Feel and Style

Possibly the most important information to convey to musicians is the proper feel of your song. Here, language is essential, because there are many ways for a musician to interpret a particular style. It is necessary to accurately describe the kind of rythmic feel you want. For example, there are many variations of the halftime feel. When you ask for a Don Williams halftime, a drummer will usually use a cross stick on the 2 and 4 beats, and play a pattern of sixteenth notes on the snare and hi-hat with his brush.

It is a good idea to talk to the musicians around town, especially drummers, and learn what they call different musical techniques and styles. If there is a situation where you have a variation of a standard feel, you will need to know what techniques to ask of the drummer.

For example, *cross stick* is the correct term for the sound when a drummer holds a stick sideways and clicks it on the rim of the snare. However, many people call this technique a "rimshot." Actually, a rimshot is a hard hit on the snare close to the rim, for dynamically loud sections. Eddie Bayers makes a good point, however. He said, "It would be nice if everyone used correct terms for drumming techniques, but if the person who hired you is calling cross sticking a rimshot, then that's what it's called."

There are so many sounds available to musicians, it can only help to learn some of the language that will accurately describe what you are hearing for your song.

4/4 Common Time

A majority of popular music on the radio these days is written in some form of 4/4, or common time. In formal music notation, the symbol: ℂ, stands for Common Time. Of course, there are many ways to play 4 quarter notes per measure. The following feel descriptions may be helpful ways to talk about a particular groove you may have in mind for your song.

Straight Feel or "Eighths"

A straight feel implies a rigid, straight quarter or eighth note feel. The term "Eighths" usually means a straight eighth note pattern on the hi-hat and rhythm instruments. Some examples of "straight eighths" are: *Tequila Sunrise*, by the Eagles and *Swinging*, by John Anderson. *He Stopped Loving Her Today*, by George Jones could be called an "Eighths Ballad".

Rock

When you use the term "Rock," a drummer usually will play the pattern in Figure 53:

Figure 53

Rock Eighths

Rock eighths also implies a straight eighths rhythmic feel. Songs such as *Wipe Out*, by The Safaris and *Heart of Rock and Roll*, by Huey Lewis would be described as rock eighths. Also, *Achy Breaky Heart*, by Billy Ray Cyrus, and *Pink Cadillac*, by Bruce Springsteen have a straight eighths rock feel.

Two Four 2/4

2/4 is often used when charting a faster 2 beat feel. This time signature is counted: "1 and 2 and, 1 and 2 and."

Figure 54

| 2/4 | 1
Wish that
1 & 2 &
One Measure | 1
I was
1 & 2 & | 4
on old
1 & 2 & | 1
Rocky Top
1 & 2 & |

2/4 usually suggests that the bass drum kicks on beats 1 and 2, and the snare hits on the "and," or upbeats. Many times a song with a **2/4** or ¢ feel will have the drummer use a *"train beat"* like in Figure 55 below. The drummer is playing sixteenth notes on the snare, but still accents the upbeats.

Figure 55

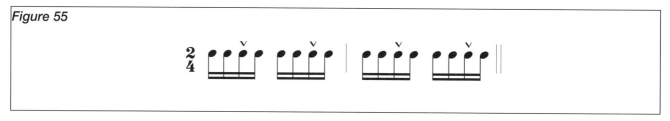

Swing

This describes a groove with a real bounce or lilt. Instead of a straight eighth note feel: ♫♫ ♫♫ , you have more of a triplet feel: ♫ ♫ ♫ ♫ . The first 2 bars of the melody for *In the Mood*, by DukeEllington, would be written like Figure 56.

Figure 56

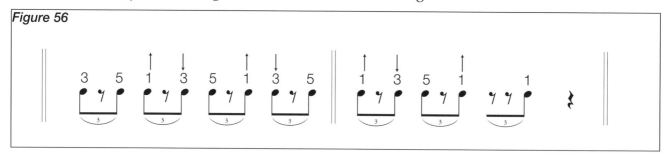

Texas Swing usually implies a **2/4** feel on drums with a 2 beat bass pattern. You'd probably write most Texas Swing charts in **2/4** . There's a real obvious 2 feel, ("1 and 2 and"), as opposed to 2 Beat Shuffles that have a definite 4 beat feel to them. Ususally, it's how you emphasize the back beat that defines the groove. On a *2 beat swing*, in **2/4** , the bass often plays the *1* and *5* notes of the chord on beats 1 and 2 of each measure. The rhythm guitar usually plays the rhythm pattern with accents on the upbeats or backbeats.

31

Of course, there are many varieties of Texas Swing. The Bob Wills song, *Deep Water* has a 2 beat feel on the verses and *walks* with a 4 beat feel (plays quarter notes through the chord changes) on the choruses. *Miles and Miles of Texas* and *San Antonio Rose* also have a swinging **2/4** feel with the bass playing the **1** and **5** notes of each chord change. You could also call this style a *2 beat swing,* since the bass and bass drum are emphasizing beats 1 and 2 of each **4/4** measure. Listen to some Asleep At The Wheel records for good examples of Texas Swing.

Shuffle

This describes a type of swing that isn't quite as exaggerated as the Texas Swing. There are many types of shuffles. *On the Other Hand*, by Randy Travis, is a medium slow country shuffle. It is a 2 beat shuffle with the bass playing on the beats 1 and 3 of each measure.

Ray Price developed such a style of shuffle, that the "Ray Price Shuffle" implies a walking bass and a jazzy, behind the beat feel. *Born To Lose* is an excellent example of a "Ray Price Shuffle." Often on a Price Shuffle, the band will play some version of Figure 57.

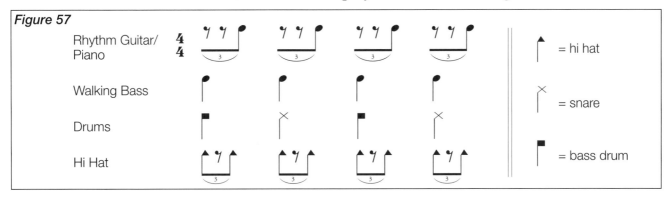

Rock Shuffle

Memphis and *Guitar Boogie* are examples of a country rock shuffle. Another good example of a rock shuffle would be *Born to Boogie*, by Hank Williams, Jr. As far as pop songs, *Heartache Tonight*, by the Eagles, could be called a rock shuffle. The song *Rosanna*, by Toto is a heavier rock shuffle, with a halftime feel. *Kansas City* is more of a *blues shuffle,* like *Boogie Shuffle* on the String Of Pearls cd. It helps to have an idea what kind of shuffle you're asking for, and if possible, to have a couple of song titles that have a similar feel what you're wanting to describe.

Cut Time

In cut time, you divide a **4/4** bar in half. The bar is read as **2/2**. A half note gets one beat; 2 halfnotes per bar. So, eighth notes from the same **4/4** piece are written and counted as quarter notes. As well, sixteenth notes are written as eighth notes and rhythmic notation is easier all around. One measure of regular time equals two measures of cut time.

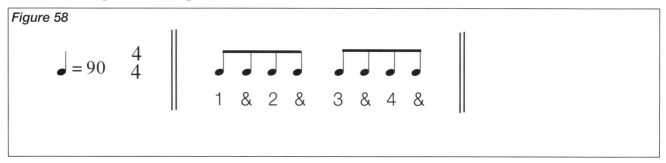
Figure 58

Figure 58 written and counted in cut time will look like Figure 59.

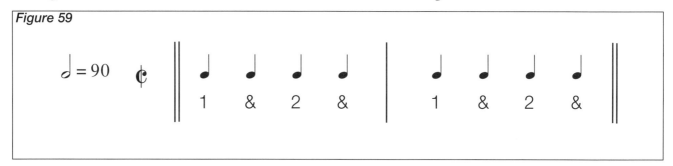
Figure 59

Cut time generally implies a song with a brisker pace and a 2 beat feel. Like **2/4**, it is also counted,"One and Two and." Most often, for a song with a halftime feel, you may write the chart in cut time.

Halftime Feel

Halftime implies a more elongated approach to the feel of a song. Instead of the snare drum, or backbeat falling on the "and" or upbeat of every measure, it falls on beats 2 and 4 of every measure. So, the time feels expanded, or longer and slower; though the actual tempo doesn't change.

Are You Sure Hank Done It This Way, by Waylon Jennings has a halftime feel. The bass guitar and bass drum hit on beats 1 2 3 & 4 and the snare on beats 2 & 4.

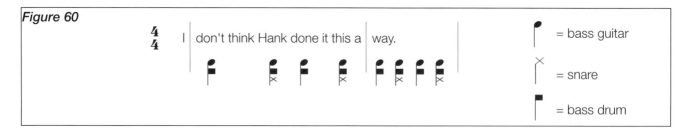
Figure 60

If you wanted to change from a halftime feel to a **2/4** feel for the chorus, you would write "2/4 feel" by the chorus section. The drummer would then hit the snare on the "ands," or upbeats. The added backbeats would give the song the faster **2/4** feel. The tempo does not change, but there are twice as many backbeats per measure.

Richie Albright, who played drums on Waylon Jenning's records in the early '70's, was the first to introduce the halftime feel into country music. Richie says he listened to "The Band" a lot, and translated some of the feels they were getting into Waylon's sound. Richie developed his own version of a halftime feel and first used it on *Lonesome, Ornery, and Mean*, then other Waylon hits around 1972 and 1973. Since, the halftime feel has become a standard approach to many country songs, and has evolved into many variations.

I'm A Ramblin' Man, by Waylon Jennings has a halftime feel. However, if the chart is written in regular time, the bass guitar and bass drum would note on every beat of the measure; beats 1, 2, 3 and 4. The snare, or backbeat would hit on downbeats 2 and 4 of each measure, instead of the "and" of each beat, thus giving the song the slower, halftime feel.

If you notated the 1st measure of the *I'm A Ramblin' Man* intro guitar lick in regular time, it would look like Figure 61.

Figure 61

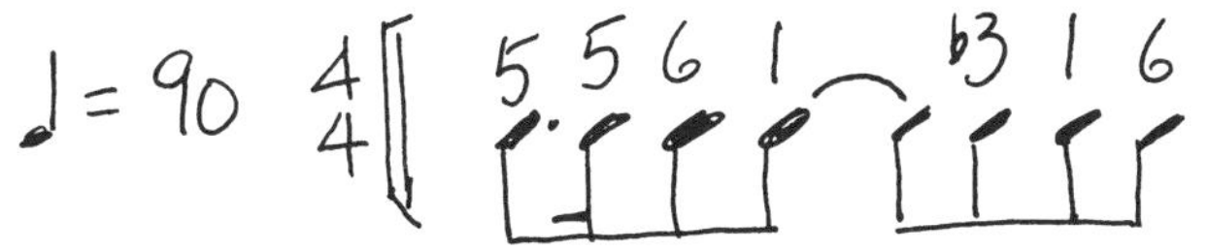

So, we can write the chart in cut time instead. The halftime feel remains because everything is played the same, but it's a lot easier to subdivide a halfnote at 90 bpm than a quarter note at 90 bpm(Fig 61). As a result, the same intro guitar lick on *I'm A Ramblin' Man*, would be written in cut time as two measures, like in Figure 62.

Figure 62

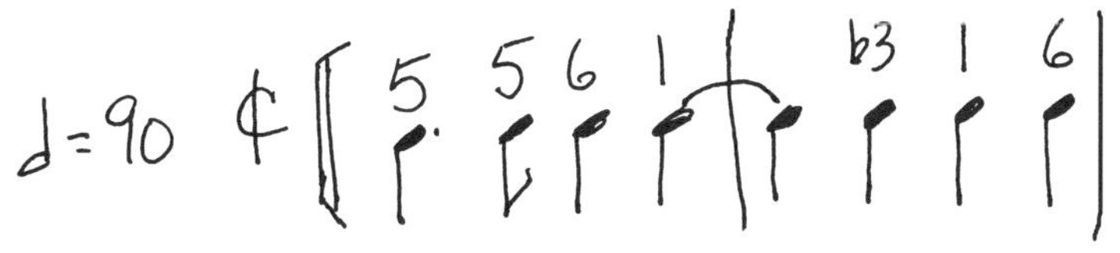

To describe the feel of *I'm A Ramblin' Man*, write Figure 63:

Figure 63

3/4 Waltz

3/4 or Waltz is a song counted with three beats per measure. There are a couple of different ways to accent a waltz. You can accent beats 2 and 3, or just beat 3.

So, the bass and bass drum would play beat 1 together then the snare and rhythm guitar would play beats 2 and 3 or beat 3 together. *Rose Colored Glasses*, by John Conlee, *Tennessee Waltz*, by Pee Wee King, and *Waltz Across Texas*, by Ernest Tubb all have the basic waltz feel of counting in "3".

6/8 Halftime Waltz

It's hard to decide whether to use **3/4** or **6/8**. **6/8** is more often done as a half time waltz, or a Waylon Jennings feel. In *the* **6/8** tune, *Mamas Don't Let Your Babies Grow Up To Be Cowboys*, by Waylon, the bass drum kicks on beat 1, and the snare hits on beat 4, while the hi-hat plays eighths. The result is the elongated half time feel shown in Figure 64.

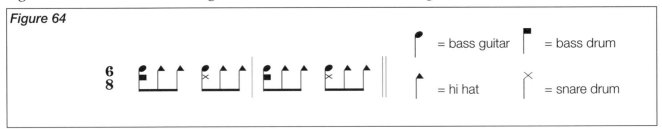

Figure 64

Ballad

When you say "ballad", you imply a more serious mood and probably a slow or medium slow eighths feel. Ballads are generally more dramatic pieces of music like, *Wind Beneath My Wings*, by Bette Midler, or *My Way*, by Elvis. You can also have a ballad that swings with a triplet feel. *You Gave Me A Mountain*, also by Elvis is a ballad with triplet feel. It feels like a slow shuffle until the end, where it really pounds out the triplets and feels almmost like **12/8**.

Triplet Feel

Figure 65 could be described as **12/8** or a slower **4/4**. The hi-hat and rhythm guitars might play a triplet figure, while the bass and bass drum thump out beats 1 and 3. The snare would hit on beats 2 and 4.

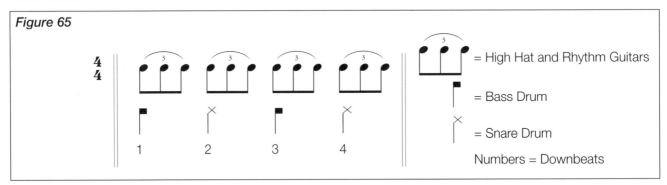

Figure 65

This is called a polyrhythm. Within the rhythm section, there are two or more separate rhythmic figures working together to create the unique triplet feel.

Some other songs that have a triplet feel are: *Blueberry Hill*, by Fats Domino, *Unchained Melody*, by The Righteous Brothers, and *Statue Of A Fool*, by Jack Greene. Use a triplet feel for a slow ballad if you want it to have a bit of a swing.

Common Mistakes

The basics for good charts are: Key Signature, Tempo, Feel, and Numbers in correct structure. If in doubt, keep it simple.

The *1* chord is not necessarily the first chord of the song. Make sure you know the tonic chord, whatever key you're in, before you label the *1* chord. For example, if your song is in the key of G, but the song starts on a C or *4* chord, make sure you don't call C the *1* chord just because it's first in the song. Also, find out what your chords are. For example, 1^{maj7} is totally different from 1^7.

There is no such thing as a $\sharp 3$ or a $\sharp 7$ chord. Also, many people accidentally write a 7 chord when they mean a $\flat 7$ chord.

If you're a bass player writing a chart, make sure to identify your chords. A "7" note to you could be a $\frac{5}{7}$ chord and not a 7 chord and the rest of the band will need to know. Also, be sure to identify major and minor chords even though they may not affect your bass note.

Complex arranging is not always best. For instance if there is a rhythm guitar lick that you want on the *1* chord and it's not important that the whole band do the lick, just write a *1*, and show the guitar player the lick. Or, you can make a side note for the guitarist instead of writing complex notation that the rest of the band doesn't need to worry about.

The *D.S. al ⊕* can be a paper saver when writing a chart, but make sure you're not adding an unnecessary degree of difficulty for those playing the chart. As well, it's difficult to read a chart where you write out only the one verse and chorus, then a whole list of instructions for the structure of the song. Usually, it's just about as easy to write out the whole song. Use repeat signs if the 1st and 2nd verse and chorus are identical, but don't repeat one line of a verse 4 times instead of writing out the whole verse.

Write your chart to emphasize phrasing. A line does not always have to be 4 measures. An extra 5th, 6th or 7th measure (whatever the song needs) used for a breath or lyric at the end of a phrase should be written at the end of that line. Start the next line of the chart with the beginning of a new phrase.

Finally, the best way to avoid an incorrect chart is play it yourself before you give it to someone else to play.

It is difficult to standardize the *Nashville Number System* because there are so many valid opinions on how to write a chart. Meanwhile, close study of this book will enable you to chart your song and have it performed just like you like it in any situation in Nashville.

String Of Pearls

String Of Pearls

String Of Pearls is a cd of 9 original instrumentals plus Amazing Grace. Each song has a different feel or time signature, so, measures are counted differently from song to song. I wrote all but one of the songs to demonstrate different types of grooves, how to understand counting bars and feeling phrases. For example, *Winter Break* is an 8ths Country Rock, *Waylon* is **6/8** with a Halftime feel and *Pelican Shuffle* is a 2 beat shuffle that goes into a 4 beat Ray Price style shuffle during the choruses.

In this chapter are descriptions of each song. Here I discuss each song's form and how my charts work. It'll be good to look at each chart and read each description as you listen to the cd. Also follow the other musician's charts to see some different approaches to charting.

Each of the 10 songs has charts handwritten by some of Nashville's best musicians:

Charlie McCoy *(Studio/Hee Haw Bandleader/Artist)*, **David Briggs** *(Studio Keyboards/Arranger/Producer)* **Jimmy Capps** *(Session Guitarist/Grand Ole Opry Staff Band)*, **Lura Foster** *(Prime Time Country/Music City Tonight/Nashville Now Chartist)*, **Brent Rowan** *(Studio Guitarist/Producer)*, **Eddie Bayers** *(Studio Drummer)*, **John Hobbs** *(Studio Keyboards/Producer)*, **Biff Watson** *(Studio Guitarist/Producer)*, **Chris Farren** *(Producer/Guitarist/Writer)*, **Tony Harrell** *(Studio Keyboardist)* and **Mike Chapman** *(Studio Bassist)*.

For example, song *#1- String Of Pearls* has charts written by: **Charlie McCoy, Brent Rowan, John Hobbs, Jimmy Capps and Biff Watson**. Song *#6- Waylon*, has charts written by **Tony Harrell, Lura Foster, Chris Farren, Biff Watson and Eddie Bayers**. The table of contents lists the charts each player has written and their page numbers. The idea is that you'll be able to compare, side by side, some of the different styles of notation and symbols you can use to chart the same piece of music. As you listen to a song on the cd, you can flip between different charts written of the same song. These different charts represent the kinds of numbering techniques that you are liable to run into in almost all of the major recording and television studios, clubs, showcases, rehearsal halls, and other situations where music is performed in Nashville.

You may or may not have heard of all the musicians who wrote charts for these songs. At the end of the charts chapter, there is a short bio of each musician taken from an interview. A lot of the recording credits for the contributing musicians are from a web site called,"**Allmusic.com**". I encourage you to visit this site and learn more about the many records these musicians have played on and produced.

<u>*String Of Pearls*</u> is also an **Extended CD (CD ROM)**. As well as high quality audio that will play in your cd player, you can insert the disk into your computer and watch animated number charts as you listen to the songs. There is a click track with each song and a highlight moving from chord to chord in time with the music. You can see exactly how to count each measure in real time with the music. Counting bars is probably the hardest part of the number system to teach. With this cd rom, you will be able to *see, hear and feel* how these charts work.

1. String Of Pearls p.c45

This is a bluegrass song. It's in a **2/4** time signature. Each measure has 2 beats or 2 quarter notes. The guitar plays a beat and a half of pickup notes by itself to lead in to the first Verse, then the band comes in on the downbeat. You play the first Verse and Chorus with the first ending. When you get to the repeat sign after the first ending, go back to the first repeat sign at the beginning of the Verse. This will be the second Verse and Chorus. From the second Verse, play through the second Chorus, but skip the first ending and play the second ending.

Now we're at the Bridge. My intention was to slow things down and have a section with a lot of feeling. I wanted almost a rubato feel (a piece of music where there is no time being counted). So, I slowed the click and practically ignored it.

Notice how in the first line of the Bridge, second measure, the "**1 diamond**" is tied to the next two bars, but the diamond is not redrawn. In this case, you strike the **1 chord** and let it ring for the three measures. In line three, you strike the **5 chord** and let it ring for four and a half measures. The diamonds for the tied chords are implied with the tie. Aside from the bridge, this is a pretty basic bluegrass chart.

2. Uncle John's Cabin p.c51

This song would be described as 8ths rock. It's a fairly fast straight rock feel. The Chorus has a pretty syncopated groove, so I wrote the rhythm. The only thing unusual about counting these measures is the last bar of the Chorus. It's a **2/4** bar and I've circled it, as well as put 2 quarter notes to show only 2 beats. There are already a lot of boxes in the Chorus, so the circle really stands out and brings attention that it is a **2/4** measure. After the Chorus, you repeat back to Verse 1, then you read on to the end of the song. There is no second ending.

In the 3rd bar of the bridge, I just used an 8th note on the ♭**7 chord** to show the pushed lick into bar 4. The rest of the measure is the Bridge groove. Also, look at the 8th bar of the Bridge. That is a band unison lick. Later, bars 15 and 16 contain a lick for the guitars that is written out to the side and circled. The asterisk indicates that the lick shows up again later in the song. I circled the lick because a box would have made it look like another measure. The rhythm section just plays the two bars of "**4 diamond**". At this point in the song, I could have written DS al Coda, but decided that it would be simpler if I went ahead and made this a 2 pager, even though the next 3 sections are the same as in the first part of the chart.

Breakdown (BRKDN): The song kind of hovers here for a minute to catch it's breath, then slams on to the end. The asterisk refers to the previous lick in the circle from page one. Even though the lick in the Bridge is elongated and modified a little from what I wrote out, I figure whoever is playing it will hear the recording and make the adjustment without too much trouble.

So, at the end, there are 2 Choruses back to back (1 Chorus with repeats). For the repeated Chorus, you skip the first ending and play the second ending. Notice the 2 quarter notes to get to the last chord.

3. White Hardware p.c60

This song is named after my grandfather's hardware store in Uniontown, Alabama. He told me that the tree behind the store grew there because someone had spit a peach pit out the window.

Anyway, this song is counted in Cut Time. Cut Time is where **4/4** is cut in half and is counted as **2/2**. In other words, 2 half notes per measure is how the basic pulse of this song feels. The kick drum is hitting on beat one and the snare on beat 2. This gives the song an elongated, half time feel. Since the tempo is one half note = 96 bpm, quarter notes will be going by at 192 bpm. So, if this song was in **2/4** and the snare was on beat 2 it would feel like a bluegrass breakdown.

Take a look at the pushes on the 2nd and 4th bars of the Verse. They are all half note pushes, so I just used a sign to designate that.

Let's follow the form; after the Intro, we play the 1st Verse and Channel (Chnl). Repeat back to the 2nd line of the intro and play the second ending.

We're at the Bridge now and play to the box that says DS al Coda. As described in the DS chapter on page 24, we go back up the chart to the Sign (2nd line of the Intro) and play until we get to the Coda (bar 20 of the 3nd Verse). From the Coda at the 3rd Verse, we skip down to the connecting Coda at the last Channel. This is really a double Channel used to jam a little.

At the Outro, we play the Intro rhythm figure 4 times and end on the **1 chord**. I normally would have witten the whole outro, but I ran out of paper.

4. Perfume & Bubblegum p.c67

Anyone who has or knows a teenage girl, knows what this song is about. That being said, what we have here is an 8ths ballad. There is a **2/4** bar in the intro, which I've boxed and put 2 hash marks over. This **2/4** bar basically serves as a set up for a spacious **"4 split 4 diamond"** which gives you a rest before starting the Verse. I could have written those 2 measures as a **"5 split 4"**, then a **2/4** bar of **"4 diamond"**, but the **4 chord** functions as an entity of it's own and not the back half of another measure. This is what I mean about phrasing.

So, we have Verse, Channel, Chorus, Bridge and 1st ending before repeating to the top of the chart and Verse 2. Once we get to the 7th bar of the 2nd Bridge, we skip the 1st ending and play the 2nd ending. This is a diamond that sustains for 2 bars and you can see that the **"5 over 7 diamond"** is tied to the 2nd bar of **"5 over 7"**.

Alright, **M8** is short for Middle 8, even though my Middle 8 is 11 bars long. It's kind of another musical adventure section and doesn't ususally happen but once in a song. Check out bar 8 of the M8; It's a bar of **3/4**. I circled the bar to bring attention to the fact that we have something different to count. Also, the 3 quarter notes show that there are only 3 beats in the measure. A measure must contain no more or no less than the amount of notes or rests defined by the time signature. So, three quarter notes in a bar of a **4/4** song would have to mean a bar of **3/4** or a mistake; that's a heads up either way.

5. Claire and Calvin p.c74

When I started writing songs for this record, I was trying to keep them simple to demonstrate number system techniques. Claire and Calvin got away from me a little bit in that respect. This song is in 4/4, but has a half time feel. In the Chorus, the snare is generally played on beat 2, which gives the half time feel. Sometimes Larry pushes the snare a sixteenth note early, like on the 1st bar of each line of the Chorus. It gives the song a cool feel as opposed to playing the snare on the "and" of every beat.

You may hear the band take some liberties with what is written. For example, Tony didn't play the sixteenth pushes with his keyboards on the 1st verse. He just played the 2nd chords of the measure directly on the downbeat. David also added a lot of his own improvisations on bass in a lot of places, instead of staying rigidly with what was written. With the other musicians adding their own interpretations, the sum is greater than anything I could have written out.

In the 1st Verse, there is a band unison lick that I have circled. There is an asterisk because the lick shows up again on the outro. Also, like we saw before in *Uncle John's Cabin*, the asterisk shows that the lick is a separate item and not another measure.

The Chorus is complicated to write out. Let's look at the 1st bar of the chorus. I wrote 2 hash marks over the **5 chord** and there is a sixteenth note push to the **6 minor**. That leaves an implied quarter note duration for the **4 chord**. On measure 2, the **2 minor** gets 2 hash marks and the 2nd chord has a sixteenth push. Those aren't hash marks on the 2nd chord. That is a "**1 eleven over 5 chord**".

At the end of the Chorus, is a repeat with 1st and 2nd endings. After the 2nd ending, there are instructions to modulate up to the **4 chord** for the Bridge. In other words, whatever the **4 chord** is in the key of D, will now be the **1 chord** in the key of G. It's tricky because, the 1st chord of the Bridge is a **6 minor**. So, the first chord of the Bridge is an **E minor**. Here is a good reason to look over a chart before you play it and make mental notes of any difficult sections, especially modulations.

After the last measure of the Bridge, we modulate back to the original key for the 3rd Verse. Next is the Middle 8. This time the Middle 8 really is 8 measures. After the Middle 8 is a verse type section dynamically, but with a different feel and chords. It's not really like any of the other Verses, but fuctions like one, building tension to be released by the Chorus.

The last Chorus is like the 2nd Chorus, but with the 2nd ending. We again modulate to the **4 chord** for the last Bridge and mod back to the original key for the Outro/Verse. notice the last chord has an 8th note instead of a sixteenth note push.

6. Waylon p.c79

Waylon Jennings really built a strong style using half time feels. This song is in **6/8** with a halftime feel similar to Waylon's song,"Mama's Don't Let Your Babies Grow Up To Be Cowboys".

On the intro, each bar gets 6 eighth notes. Then there's the 3rd bar, which is half a bar and only gets 3 eighth notes. It's a **3/8** measure and I've boxed it in and placed hash marks, just like I would for a **2/4** bar in a **4/4** song. The 4th bar is again in **6/8** and is a diamond tied to the next **3/8** measure. For the intro piece, I wanted a lot of feel. I had the click track going so the band could all come in together, but largely ignored it for the sake of a rubato like feel on the guitar.

In the 1st Verse, there is a 9th measure. It is written after bar 8 of the Verse instead of as bar 1 of the Chorus. Measure 9 is an extra bar that gives the Verse time to finalize and then build anticipation for the Chorus. Even though it makes for an odd number of bars in the Verse, it is definitely not part of the Chorus and is written as an extra measure in the Verse.

There is nothing too unusual yet. We read to the end of the 1st Chorus and follow the repeat sign to Verse 2 where the slide solo begins and continues through the Chorus.

The Turnaround is just like the Intro, but afterward we modulate down a whole step to the key of C for the Bridge.

Notice that the 1st chord of the Bridge is a **4 chord**. This chord is an *F major 7 six nine*, because it's a major 7 with a G and D note.

Check out bar 17 of the Bridge. This is another example of an extra measure that finishes the phrase of the 4th line instead of being placed at the beginning of the 5th line of the Bridge.

After the 5th line, 2nd measure of the Bridge, the song modulates back up a whole step to the original key for a double Chorus build.

The Outro is just like the Intro, but Ritards slightly into the final chord.

7. Boogie Shuffle p.c86

This is a blues shuffle and called a boogie because the rhythm guitar rocks back and forth between the 5 and 6 note of the chord. The slide guitar has 3 1/2 beats of pickup notes before the downbeat of the song. So, the drummer would need to give the slide guitarist a 2 bar count. In time, he would say,"one (rest), two (rest), one, two, three, four." The slide guitar starts his pickup notes on the "and" of the 2nd "one". The band comes in on the downbeat following "four". (The drummer doesn't really say,"*rest*".)

There are only 8th note pushes in this song, so the push sign will work throughout the tune. Notice bar 3. The **1 chord** is played on the "and" of beat 2 and the ♭**7 chord** is played right on beat 4. Bar 5 of the Intro is a unison lick played by the whole band and is in a box. It is a bar to be played by everyone and not just as a guitar lick.

After Verse 1 and Chorus 1, we play the 1st ending, repeat and play the 2nd ending; then on to the Bridge.

This chart plays on from the Bridge with nothing unusual until the last Chorus, where bar 9 is just like the first bar of the Intro, yet is also the last bar of the Chorus. I could have written the last 3 bars of the Chorus as the first 3 bars of the Outro, but they feel more like part of the Chorus at that point instead of starting an Outro section. It feels right calling the **4 chord** lick the outro because of the way it's phrased. There is a quarter note rest before the last chord just because...

8. Winter Break p.c93

Here is another boogie song, but it is straight 8ths instead of a shuffle. It could be called an 8ths Boogie. The song is in the key of A, but the Choruses are in E. I wrote and circled the new keys in front of each section that modulated just as a courtesy. Notice in Charlie McCoy's version, he didn't modulate on the choruses. He continued to write in the original key.

For the Intro, there are 2 bars of rhythm guitar pickups before the lead guitar comes in with the melody of the 1st Verse. At the end of the Verse, "Mod ↘ to 5" means modulate to the **5 chord** (E) of the original key (A), so that the new **1 chord** is now E; **5=1**. However, the 1st chord of the Chorus is a **5 chord** in the new key. So, even though we're now in the key of E, the 1st chord of the Chorus is a **B chord**.

Look at bar 8 of the Chorus. There are 3 eighth notes showing the rhythm played for the 2nd part of the split bar. If there is no other rhythmic notation in a split bar, it is assumed that the rest of the bar gets regular rhythm until the notation on the second half of the bar. So, for syncopated split bar 8, you play the **1 chord** until beat 3, and play the ♭**7 chord** on the "and" of beat 3 with the rhythm notated. All this is to say that in a measure like this, the rhythm of the 1st chord of the bar is implied and does not need to be written out to understand the measure.

The only thing different with the rest of the song is the last measure. Here, the **4 chord** gets 4 eighth notes, so we know that the **5 chord** in that bar lasts for 2 beats instead of 2 1/2 beats.

9. Pelican Shuffle p.c99

This song gets into a couple of different types of shuffles. The Verses use a 2 beat country shuffle and the rest of the song is in a 4 beat or Ray Price Shuffle. In the 2 beat shuffle, the bass is playing on beats 1 and 3 and the rhythm instruments are accenting backbeats 2 and 4.

When you get to the Ray Price Shuffle, the bass and left hand of the piano player begin walking (usually playing the: **1, 3, 5, 3** notes of each chord on beats 1, 2, 3 and 4). The rhythm instruments (piano [right hand] and guitar in this song) play the chord changes on the "and" of each beat.

From the Verse, the chart reads through the Chorus to bar 14: **"5 Stop with a 2 Beat Rest"**.

After the stop, the rhythm resumes in a 2 beat feel as instructed in the 1st ending. From the repeat, the 2 beat feel continues through the 2nd Verse. When we get to the 2nd Chorus, it's Ray Price again for the 2nd ending of the Chorus and the rest of the song.

In the Bridge, there is a rhythmic lick at the first part of the 1st bar, then regular rhythm resumes for the rest of the measure. I only notated the 8th notes and placed hash marks to show that regular rhythm finishes each bar.

The last Chorus is similar to the others, except bars 15 and 16, which are just different chords that take us to the Tag. The Tag basically restates the Intro lick which is followed by the ending.

10. Amazing Grace p.c105

This is the other song with a "Three Beat" feel on this record. It has a **3/4**, waltz feel and modulates several times. The Intro and 1st Verse are rubato and there is no countable time between chord changes. I just played how I felt it and tried to get each guitar chord to have it's own space to resonate.

The last bar of the Verse, like the Intro is a fermata, aka a "Birds Eye". There is no way to count this chord that's held like a diamond. So, the band (rhythm guitar in this case) waits for a cue, which is the 1st note of the melody; a quarter note pickup by the dobro. This pickup note is also in the new key of F♯.

The 2nd Verse is just dobro and guitar until the last bar of the Verse where everyone plays the chords as written. So, the whole band is in at the asterisk. For Verse 4 we modulate up a half step to the key of G and the fiddle is introduced with a solo.

The Turnaround uses the same lick that the band came in with at the end of the 2nd Verse. The dobro plays some lead over this pattern.

For the last bar of the last Verse, the band diamonds on the **1 chord**, which sets up the Tag. Here, the guitar plays by itself, restating the last line of the Intro. The guitar then Ritards to the **"5 Bird's Eye"**. It plays the two diamonds, then cues the band so all can play the last chord together.

STRING OF PEARLS
CHART: CHAS WILLIAMS

G 2/4
♩=100
Bluegrass

|V| [: 1   5   2-   6-
     4   1   5   5
     1   5   2-   6-
     4⅓ 2⁻⁷5   1   5/7

|C| 6-   5   4   1
     6-   5   4   4
     6-   5   4   ⅓
     2   2 |1.| 2⅓ 45 :|| |2.| 2 2⅓ 4 4 4 3

|B| 6- ¼   ◇1   1   1
     6- ¼   ◇1   1   1
     6- ¼   ⅓1   2⁻⁷6- |¼| ◇5   5   5 RIT
     6- 5/7 ◇1   1   1
     6- 5/7 1 ◇4^Δ9 4^Δ9 4^Δ9
     6- 1   4^Δ9 6- 4^Δ9 ◇5/7 5/7 5/7 5/7

|V| 1   5   2-   6-
     4   1   5   5
     1   5   2-   6-
     4⅓ 2⁻⁷5 1   5/7

|C| 6-   5   4   1
     6-   5   4   4
     6-   5   4   ⅓
     2   2   2⅓   45

|V| 1   5   2-   6-
     4   1   5   5
     1   5   2-   6-
     4⅓ 2⁻⁷5 1   1

|TAG| 4⅓ 2⁻⁷5 1   1 1̂

Chas Williams

c45

CHART: Charlie McCoy

STRING OF PEARLS

[V] Acoustic
3 ⌣⌣⌣   1 5 2m 6m   4 1 5 5   1 5 2m 6m | 4 1/3 | 2m 5 | 1 5/7

[CHO] 6m 5 4 1   6m 5 4 | 4 ⌣⌣11 | 6m 5 4 1   2 2 | 2 1/3 | 4 5 |

[V2] 1 5 2m 6m   4 1 5 5   1 5 2m 6m | 4 1/3 | 2m 5 | 1 5/7

[CHO] 6m 5 4 1   6m 5 4 | 4 ⌣⌣11 | 6m 5 4 1   2 2 2 | 2 1/3 |

4 4 4   3

AD LIB
[Br] | 6m 4 ♩♩ | 1̂ ◯ | 6m 4 ♩♩ | 1̂ ◯ | 6m 4 1/3 1 ♩♩♩♩ | | 2m 6m ♩♩ | | 4 ♩ | 5̂

| 6m 5/7 ♩♩ | 1̂ ◯ | 6m 5/7 ♩♩ | 1 | 4^ ◯ | | 6m 1 ♩♩ | | 4 6m ♩♩ | | 4 ♩ | 5̂

IN TEMPO
[V3]   1 5 2m 6m   4 1 5 5   1 5 2m 6m | 4 1/3 | 2m 5 | 1 5/7

[CHO] 6m 5 4 1   6m 5 4 | 4 ⌣⌣♯ | 6m 5 4 1   2 2 | 2 1/3 | 4 5 |

[OUT] 1 5 2m 6m   4 1 5 5   1 5 2m 6m | 4 1/3 | 2m 5 | 1 1

| 4 1/3 | 2m 5 | 1   1̂
                      TTP

c46

CHART: Jimmy Capps

G 2/4
MM 100

String of Pearls

S: 1 5 2- 6-
4 1 5 5
V: 1 5 2- 6-
(4 1/3) (2-5) 1 5/7
6- 5 4 1
(Cho) 6- 5 4 4
6- 5 4 1/3
2 2 [1st] (2 1/3)(45) :||

[2nd]
2 (2 1/3) 4 4 4 3 ritard

Bridge
(6- 4/1)
(6- 4/1)
(6- 4/1)(1/3 1)(2-6-)(4/1 5) 5 5 5
(6- 5/7)
(6- 5/7)(1 4/9) 4/9 4/9 4/9
(6- 1)(4/9 6-) 4/9 5/7 5/7 5/7 5/7 D.S. Al Coda

⊕ 1 5 2- 6-
4 1 5 5
1 5 2- 6-
(4 1/3)(2-5) 1 1

Tag (4 1/3)(2-5) 1 (1 5 1 / 1 1 1)

Chart By
Jimmy Capps

STRING OF PEARLS

CHART: BIFF WATSON

G

V) | 1 5 | 2- 6- | 4 1 | 5
    | 1 5 | 2- 6- | 4 ½ 3 2-5 | 1 5/7

Chor) | 6-5 | 4 1 | 6-5 | 4 "₂5₇♭
      | 6-5 | 4 1 | | 2⁷   2½ 3 4 5 ||
                      | | 2⁷   2⁷ ⅓   4   4 3⁷ |

RUBATO

Br) | 6-¼ 1 — 1 | 6-¼ 1 — 1
    | 6-¼ 3 1 | 2- 6- ¼ 5 — 5
    | 6- 5/7 1 — 1 | 6- 5/7 1 4^Δ9 — 4^Δ9
    | 6- 1 4^Δ9 6- | 4^Δ9 5/7 | 5/7

A TEMPO

V) | 1 5 | 2- 6- | 4 1 | 5
    | 1 5 | 2- 6- | 4 ½ 3 2-5 | 1 5/7

Chor) | 6-5 | 4 1 | 6-5 | 4 "₂5₇♭
      | 6-5 | 4 ⅓ | 2⁷ | 2⁷ ⅓ 4 5

V) | 1 5 | 2- 6- | 4 1 | 5
    | 1 5 | 2- 6- | 4 ½ 3 2-5 | 1

TAG | 4 ½ 3 2-5 | 1 1 (𝄐)

CHART: John Hob[…]

STRING OF PEARLS

KEY = G
FAST 4

V1,2) 1 5 2⁻ 6⁻
4 1 5 5
1 5 2⁻ 6⁻
4 ⅓ 2⁻5 1 5/7

C) 6⁻ 5 4 1
6⁻ 5 4
6⁻ 5 4 ⅓
2 2 |1. 2⅓ 45 :|| |2. 2 2⅓ 4 4 4 3⁷

BRIDGE

6⁻ 4⁷ 1 1 1
6⁻ 4⁷ 1 1 1
6⁻ 4⁷ ⅓ 1 2⁻6⁻ 4 5 5 5 5
6⁻ 5/7 1 1 1
6⁻ 5/7 1 4² 4² 4² 4²
6⁻ 1 4² 6⁻ 4² 5²/7 5²/7

V3) 1 5 2⁻6⁻
4 1 5 5
1 5 2⁻6⁻
4 ⅓ 2⁻5 1 5/7

C3) 1 5 2⁻6⁻
4 1 5 5
1 5 2⁻6⁻
4 ⅓ 2⁻5 1 1

TAG) 4 ⅓ 2⁻5 1 1 1

c49

CHART: BRENT ROWAN

♩ = ¢

STRING OF PEARLS

A₁ 𝄋

| 1 | 5 | 2m | 6m | 4 | 1 | 5 | 5 |

| 1 | 5 | 2m | 6m | 4 1/3 | 2m⁷5 | 1 | 5/7 |

B₁

| 6m 5 | 4 | 1 | 6m | 5 | 4 | 4 |

| 6m 5 | 4 | 1/3 | 2 | 2 | 2 1/3 | 4 5 |

A₂

| 1 | 5 | 2m | 6m | 4 | 1 | 5 | 5 |

| 1 | 5 | 2m | 6m | 4 1/3 | 2m⁷5 | 1 | 5/7 |

B₂

| 6m 5 | 4 | 1 | 6m | 5 | 4 | 4 |

| 6m 5 | 4 | 1/3 | 2 | 2 | 2 | 2 1/3 |

| 4 | 4 | 4 | 3 | no tempo **C** 6m 4⁷ | 1 | 6m 4⁷ | 1 |

rit.

| 6m 4⁷ | 1/3 1 | 2m 6m | 4⁷ 5 | 6m 5/7 | 1 |

| 6m 5/7 | 1 4⁹ | 4⁷ | 6m 1 | 4 6m | 4⁹ | 5 | 5 |

BAND D.O. **D.S.** to A
rato tempo

| ¢ | 1 | 1 |

| 4 1/3 | 2m⁷5 | 1 | 1 |

c50

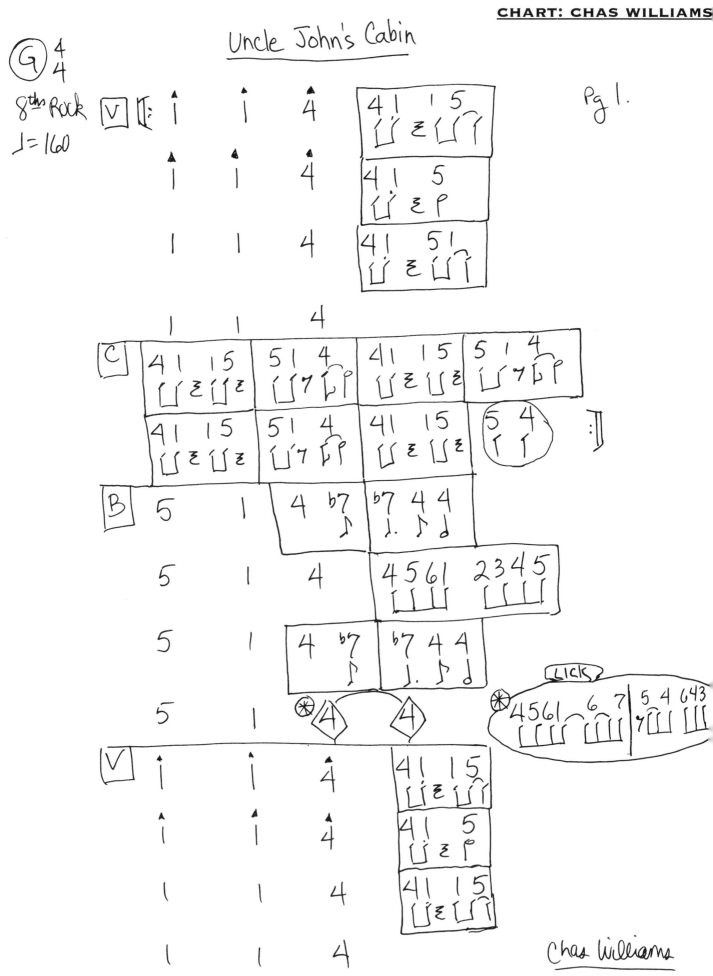

Uncle John's Cabin

CHART: CHAS WILLIAMS
Pg. 2

G 4/4

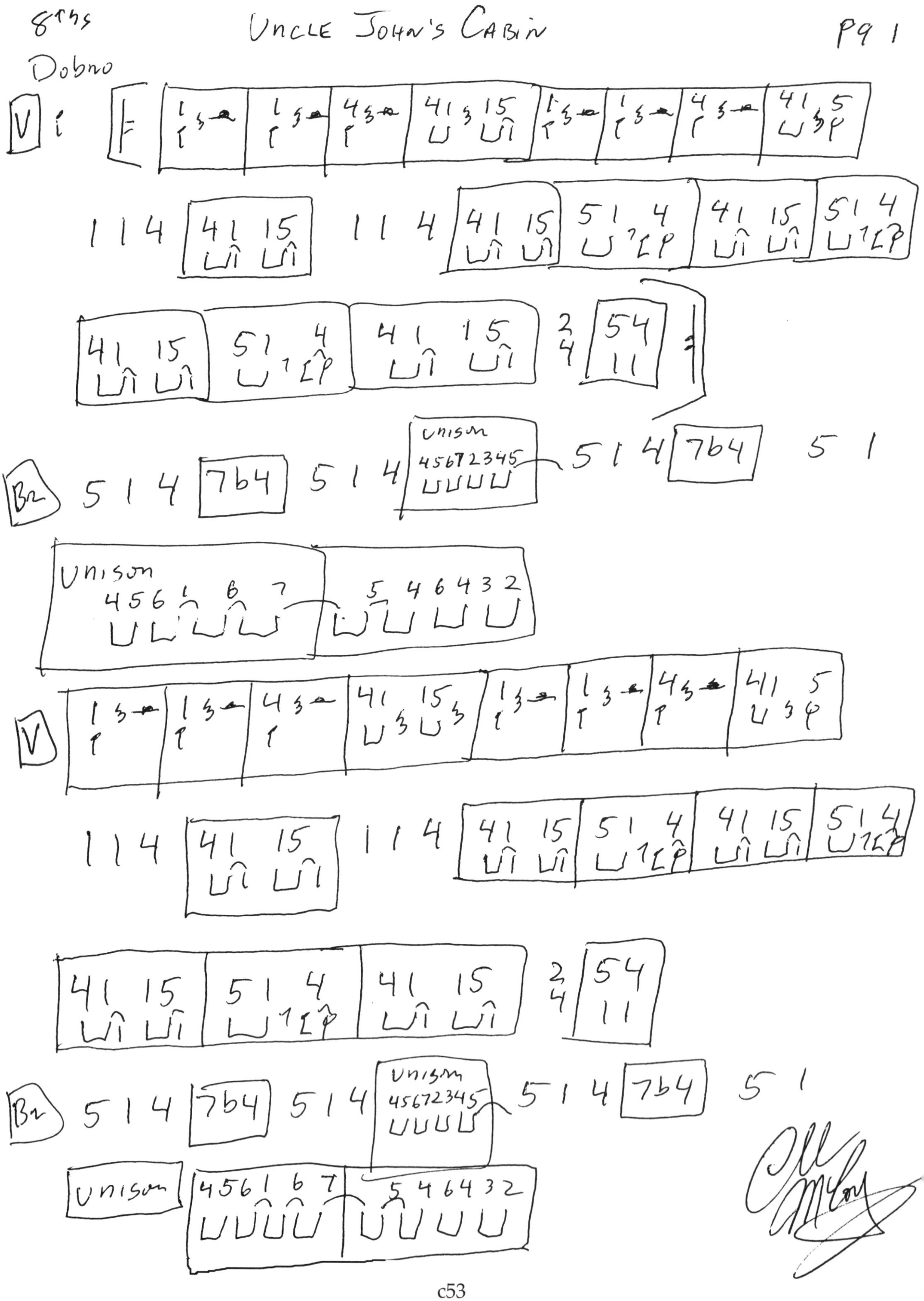
8ths
Uncle John's Cabin
Pg 1
Dobro
V
Br
unison
Unison
V
Br
unison
unison

CHART: CHARLIE McCOY

Uncle John's Cabin — pg 2

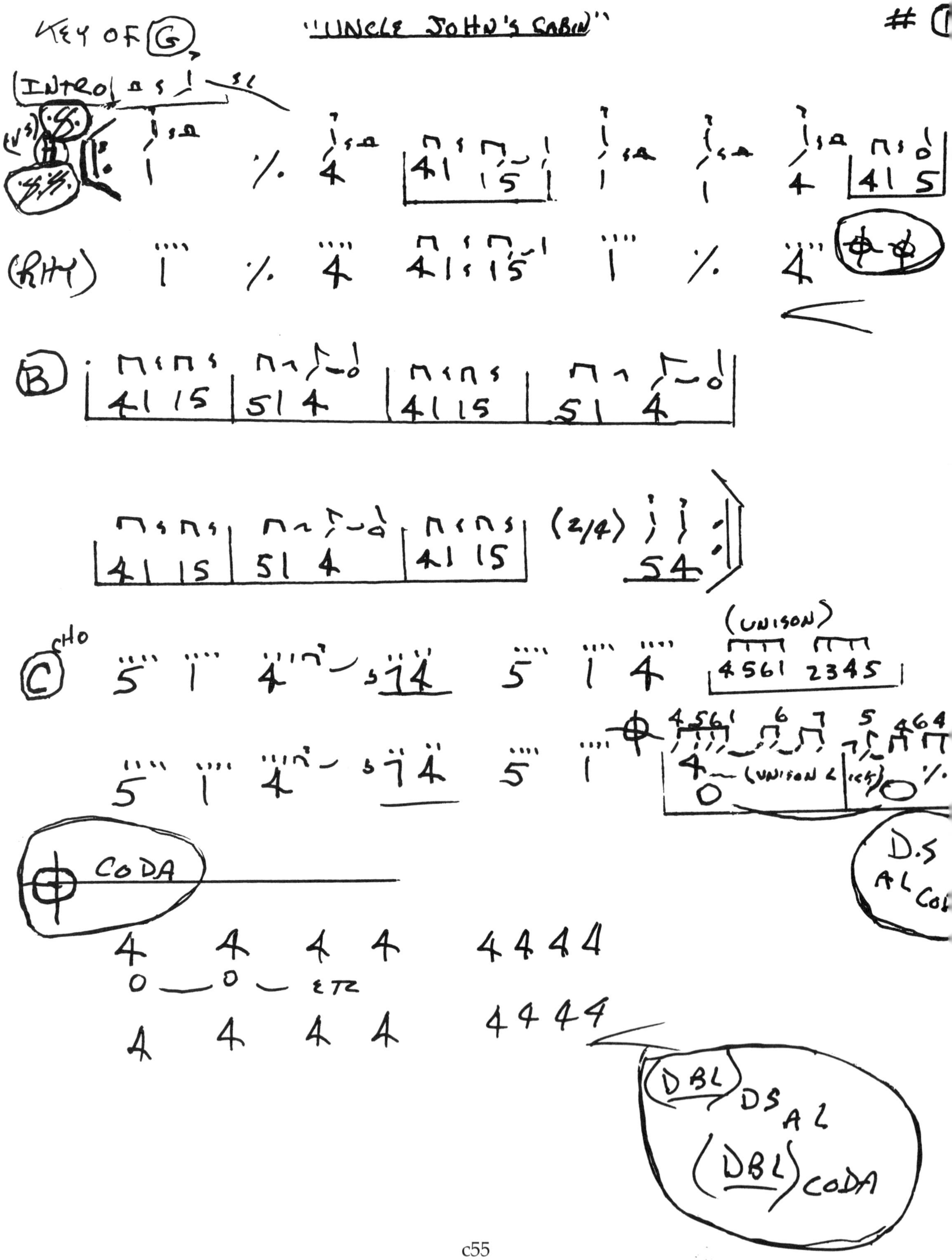
KEY OF G
"UNCLE JOHN'S CABIN"
INTRO
(RHY)
B
(2/4)
C
(UNISON)
CODA
D.S AL CO
DBL DS AL (DBL) CODA

CHART: DAVID BRIGGS

"UNCLE JOHN'S CABIN"   # ②

DBL CODA ⊕ ⊕

|: 4 1 1 5 | 5 1 4 o | 4 1 1 5 | 5 1 4 o |

| 4 1 1 5 | 5 1 4 o | 4 1 1 5 |① 5 1 4 o :|

② (2/4) 5 4   (4/4) 1̂

Uncle John's Cabin

CHART: TONY HARREL

(G) US

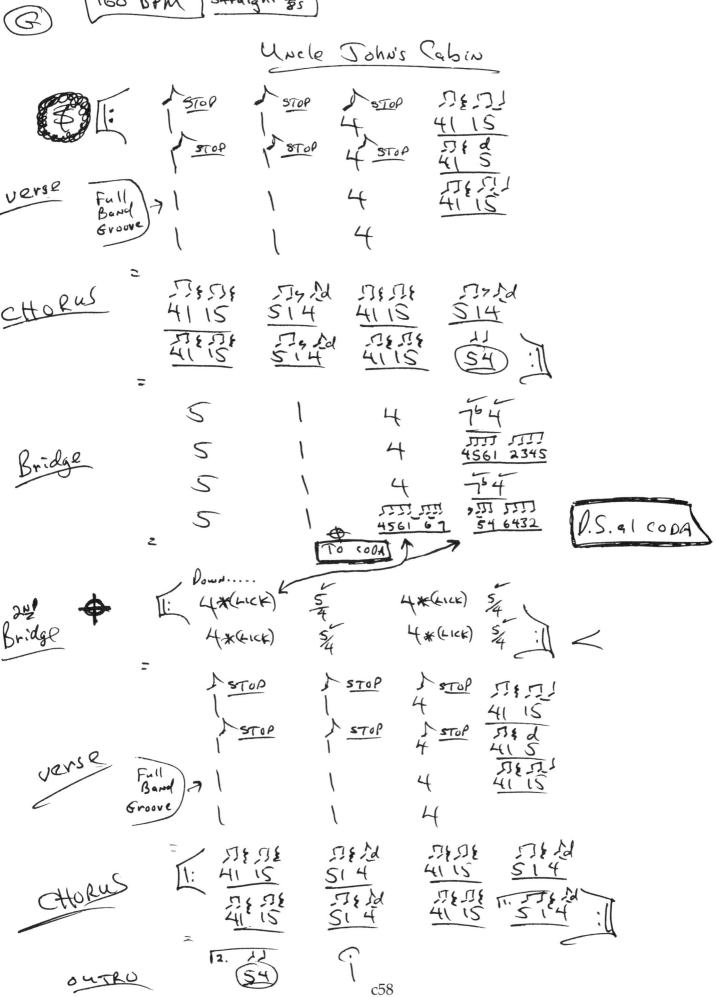

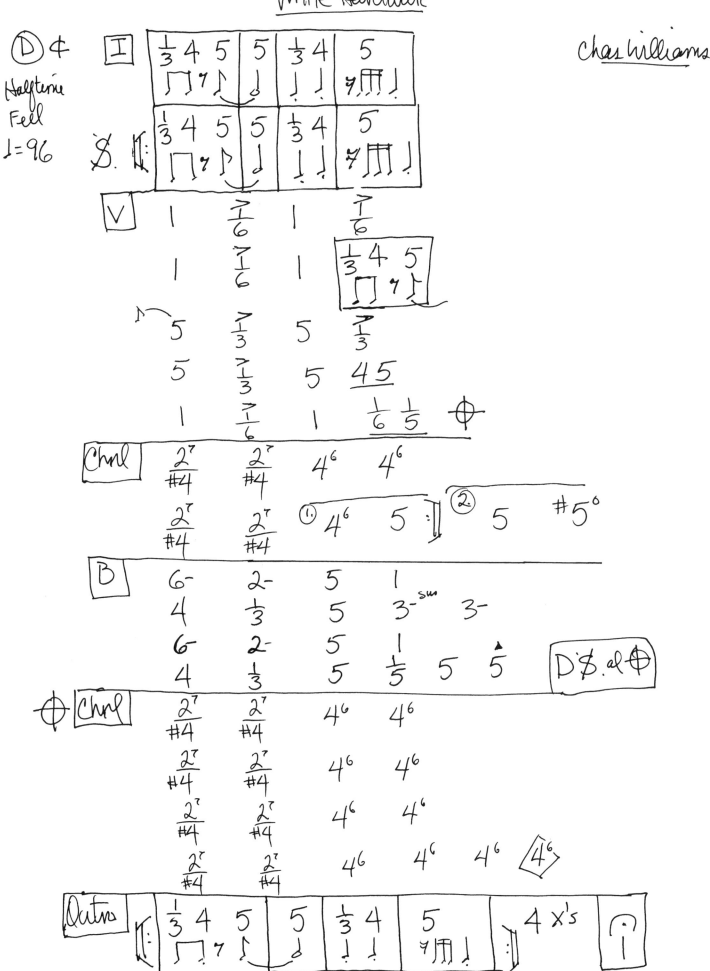

WHITE HARDWARE — LURA FOSTER

CHART: LURA FOSTE

(MORE)

WHITE HARDWARE P.2

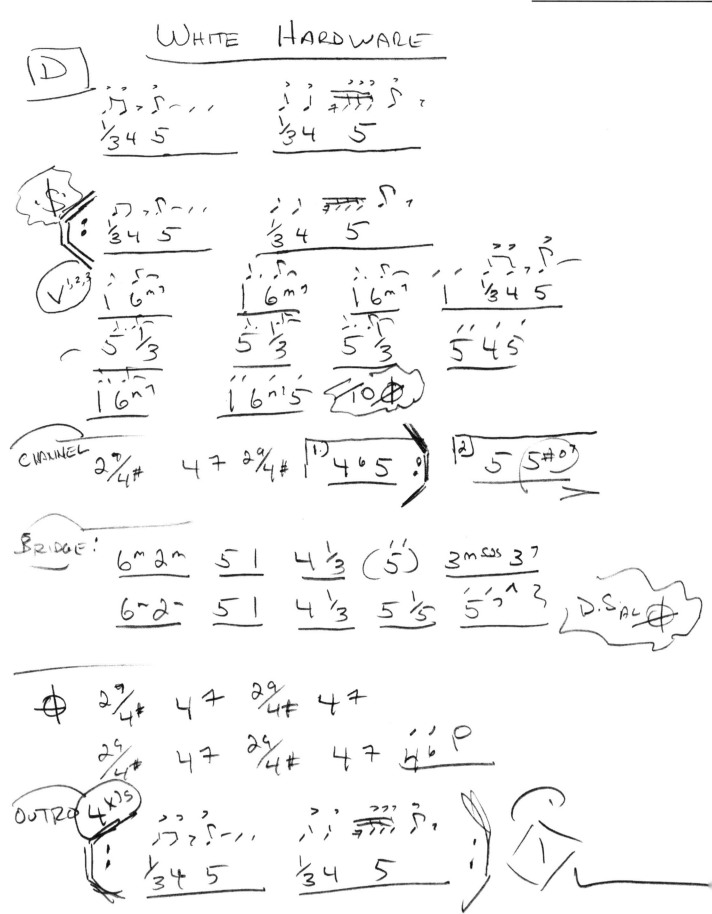

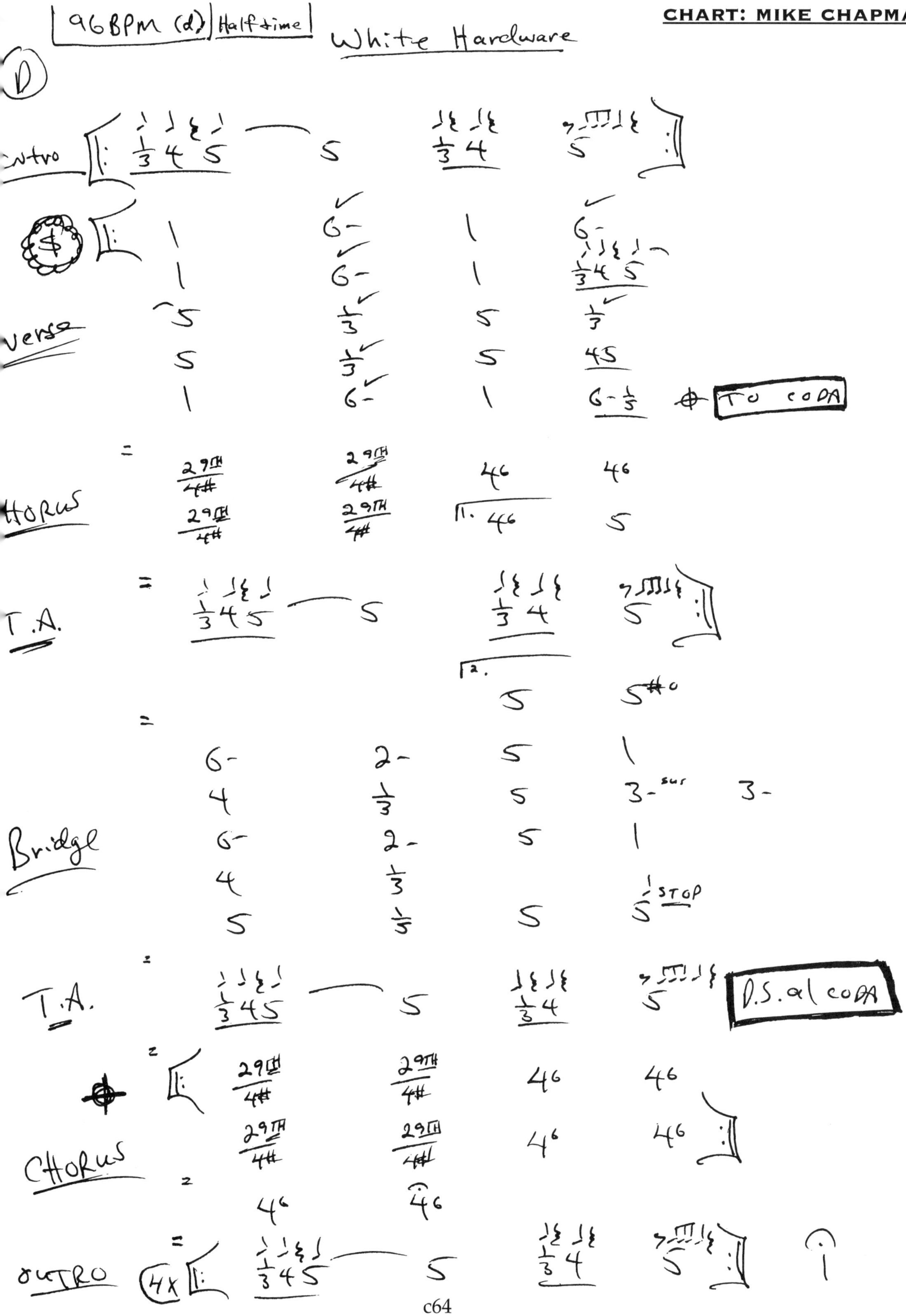

96BPM (♩) Halftime
White Hardware
D
Intro
Verse
Chorus
TO CODA
T.A.
Bridge
sus
STOP
D.S. al CODA
Chorus
Outro
4X

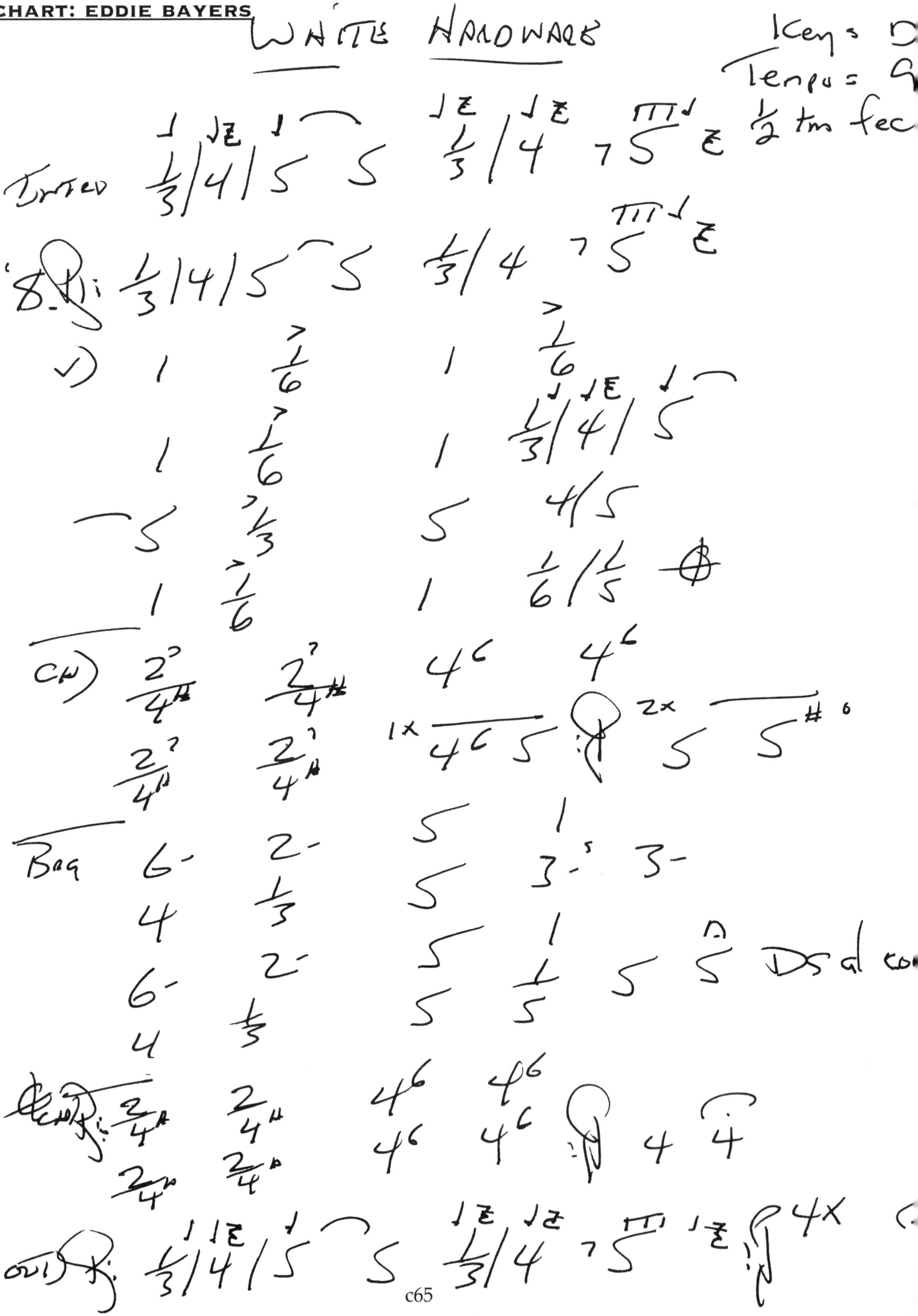

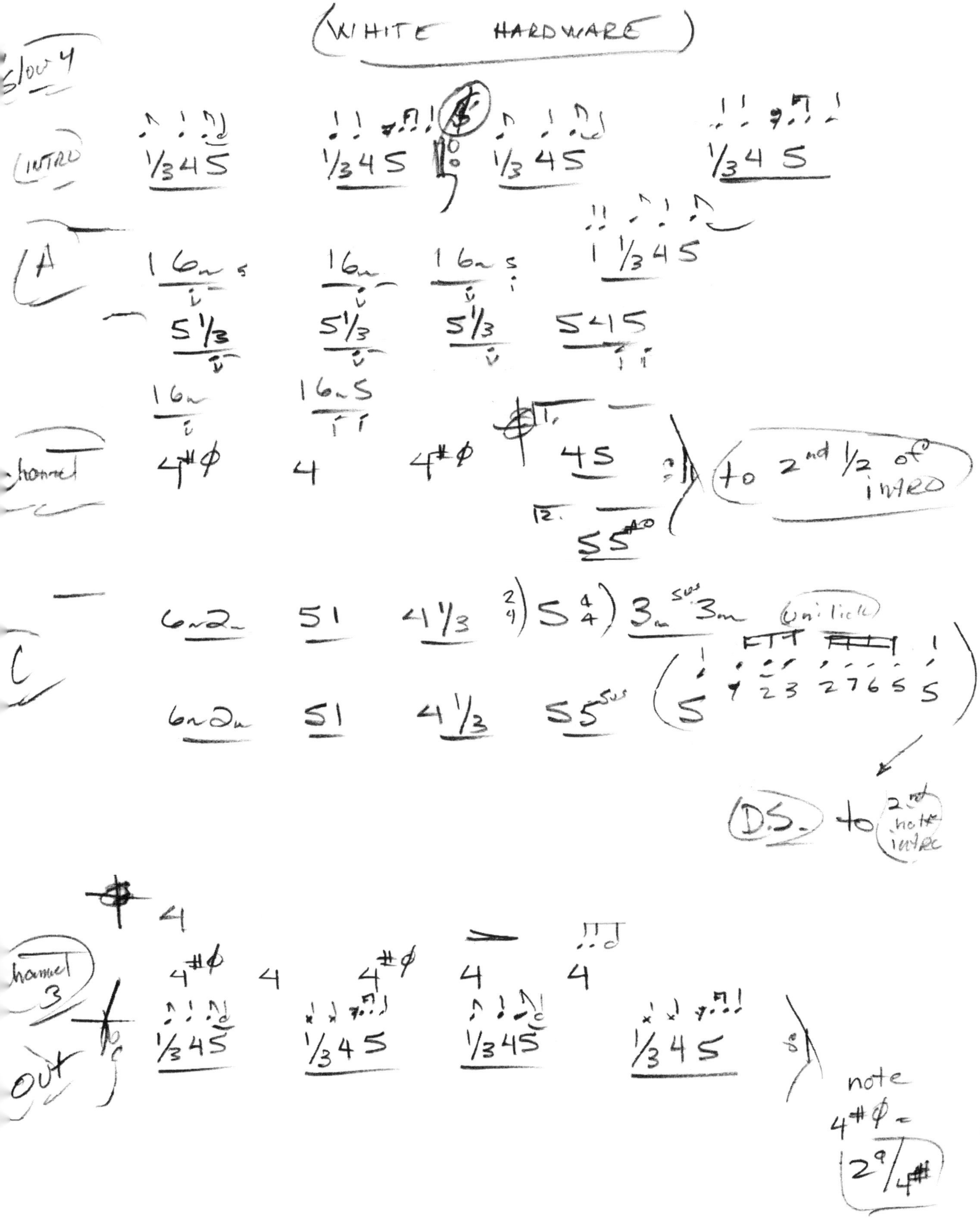
WHITE HARDWARE
Slow 4
INTRO
1/3 4 5 1/3 4 5 1/3 4 5 1/3 4 5
A
16m 16m 16m 1 1/3 4 5
5 1/3 5 1/3 5 1/3 5 4 1 5
16m 16m 5
Channel
4#Φ 4 4#Φ 4 5
5 5
to 2nd 1/2 of intro
C
6m 2m 5 1 4 1/3 5 3m sus 3m
(uni lick)
5 7 2 3 2 7 6 5 5
6m 2m 5 1 4 1/3 5 5sus
D.S. to 2nd half intro
4
Channel 3
4#Φ 4 4#Φ 4 4
OUT
1/3 4 5 1/3 4 5 1/3 4 5 1/3 4 5
note 4#Φ = 2⁹/4#

Perfume & Bubblegum

G 4/4
8ths
Ballad
♩=82

CHART: CHAS WILLIAM

| I | 1 6- | 5 4 | 1 6- | 5" | 4 ④ |

| V | 1 | 5 | 6- | 4 | |
| | 1 | 5 | 6- 3⁻⁷ | 4 5 | |

| Chnl | 4⅓ | 2⁻⁷ | 4⅓ | 2⁻⁷ |
| | 4⅓ | 2⁻⁷ 5/7 | | |

| C | 1 4⅓ | 1 5 | 1 4⅓ | ◇ |

| B | 6-5 | 4⅓ | 2⁻⁷ ¼ 6- ¼ | 5 | ① 5/7 5/7 :|| ② 5/7 5/7 |
| | 6-5 | 4⅓ | 2⁻⁷ 2⁻⁷/1 | | |

| M8 | 5/7 1 ⅓ | ¼ 0 | 5/7 1 ⅓ | 4 6- 5/7 |
| | 5/7 1 ⅓ | 6- 0 | 5/7 1 ⅓ | 2⁻⁷ 4△9 5/7 | 1 0 |

2⁻⁷ 4△9 6- ¼ | 5/7

| C | 1 4⅓ | 1 5 | 1 4⅓ | 1 5 |
| | 1 4⅓ | 1 5 | 1 4⅓ | 1 𝄢 |

Chas Williams

Perfume and Bubblegum

CHART: TONY HARRELL

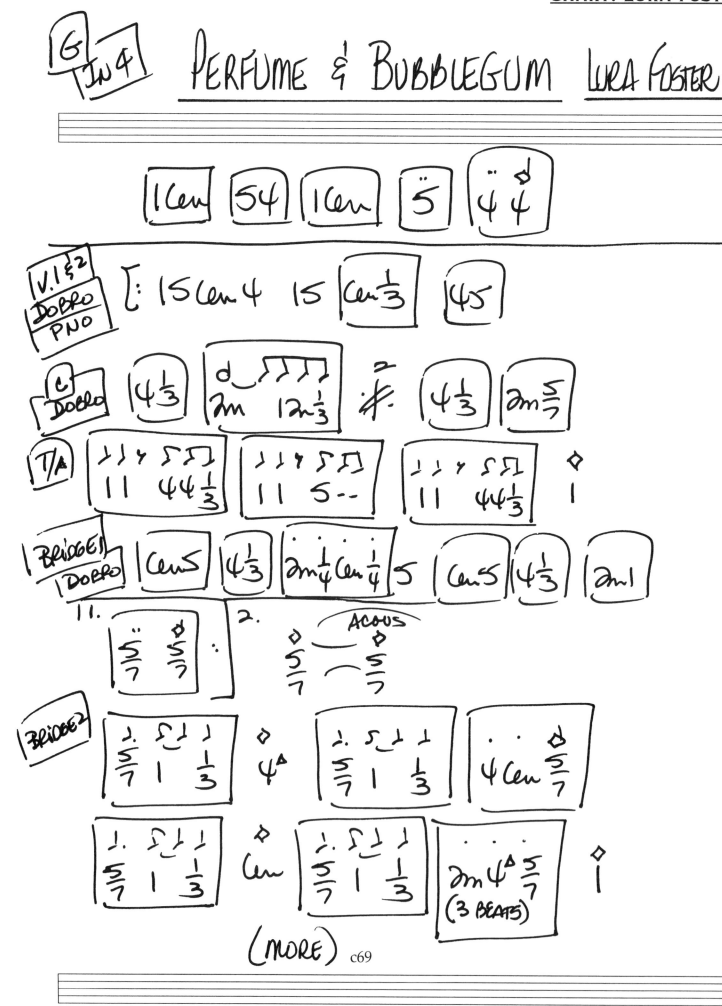

Perfume & Bubblegum   P.2

CHART: BIFF WATSON

G PERFUME + BUBBLEGUM

INTRO) | 1 6- | 5 4 | 1 6- (5) | 4"d |

V) 2.| 1² | 5 | 6- | 4 |
    | 1² | 5 | 6-3-7 | 4 5 |

CHAN) | 4 1/3 | 2-7 1²3 2TT | 4 1/3 | 2-7 1²3 2TT |
      | 4 1/3 | 2-7 5/7 ← |

CHOR) | 1 4 1/3 | 1 5 | 1 4 1/3 | 1 0 ⟩ |

REFRAIN) | 6-5 | 4 1/3 | 2-7/4 6-1/4 | 5 |
         | 6-5 | 4 1/3 | 2-7 2-7/1 | 5/7 |
         | | | | 1² 5/7 5/7 |

BRIDGE) | 5/7 1 1/3 | 1/4 | 5/7 1 1/3 | 4 6 5/7 |
        | 5/7 1 1/3 | 6- | 5/7 1 1/3 [3/4] 2-7 4♭9 5/7 [4/4] | 1 0 |
        | 2-7 4♭9 6 1/4 | 5/7 ← |

CHOR) | 1 4 1/3 | 1 5 | 1 4 1/3 | 1 5 |
      | 1 4 1/3 | 1 5 | 1 4 1/3 | ↑ 0 |

c71

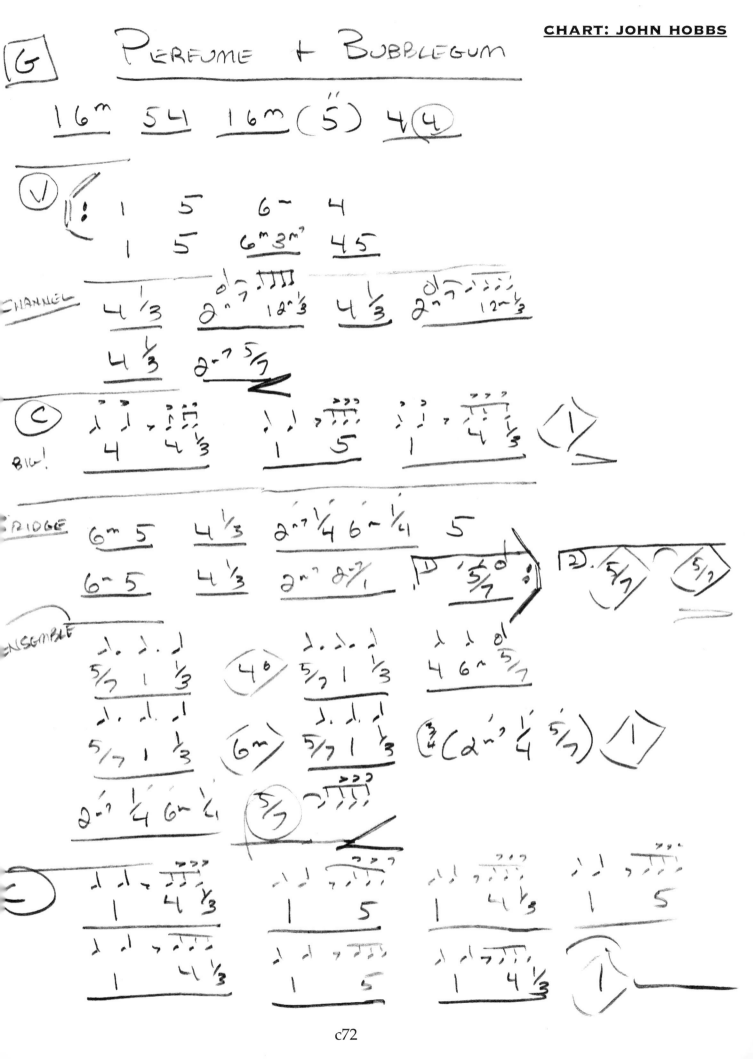

Perfume & Bubblegum

CHART: CHRIS FARRE

Intro: | 1 6m | 5 4 | 1 6m | (2/4) 5 | 4 |

V1: | 1 | 5 | 6m | 4 |
| 1 | 5 | 6m/3 | 4 5 |

B1: | 4 1/3 | 2m7 | 4 1/3 | 2m7 |
| 4 1/3 | 2m5/7 |

CH.: | 1 4 1/3 | 1 5 | 1 4 1/3 | 1 |

Bridge 1: | 6m 5 | 4 1/3 | 2m7 1/4 6m 1/4 | 5 |
| 6m 5 | 4 1/3 | 2m7 1 | 1. 5/7 : 2. 5/7 |

Bridge 2: | 5/7 1 1/3 | 4 | 5/7 1 1/3 | 4 6m 5/7 |
| 5/7 1 1/3 | 6m | 5/7 1 1/3 | 3/4 2m7 4° 5/7 | (4/4) |
| 2m7 6m 1/4 | 5 |

CH: | 1 4 1/3 | 1 5 | 1 4 1/3 | 1 5 |
| 1 4 1/3 | 1 5 | 1 4 1/3 | 1 |

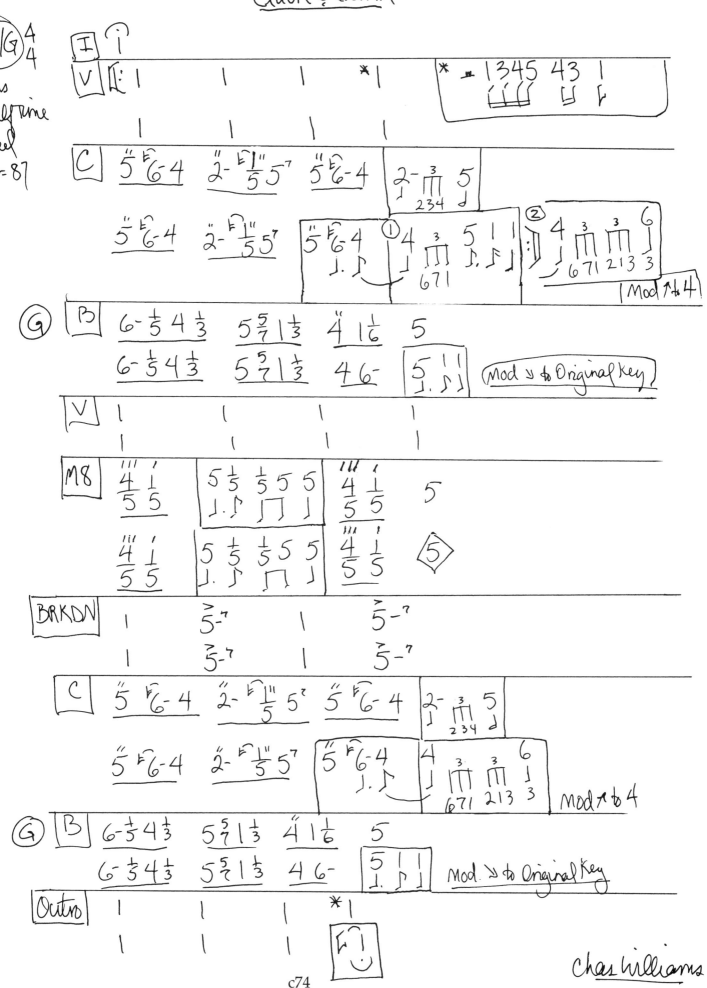

CLAIRE & CALVIN P.2

CHART: LURA FOSTER

CLAIRE + CALVIN

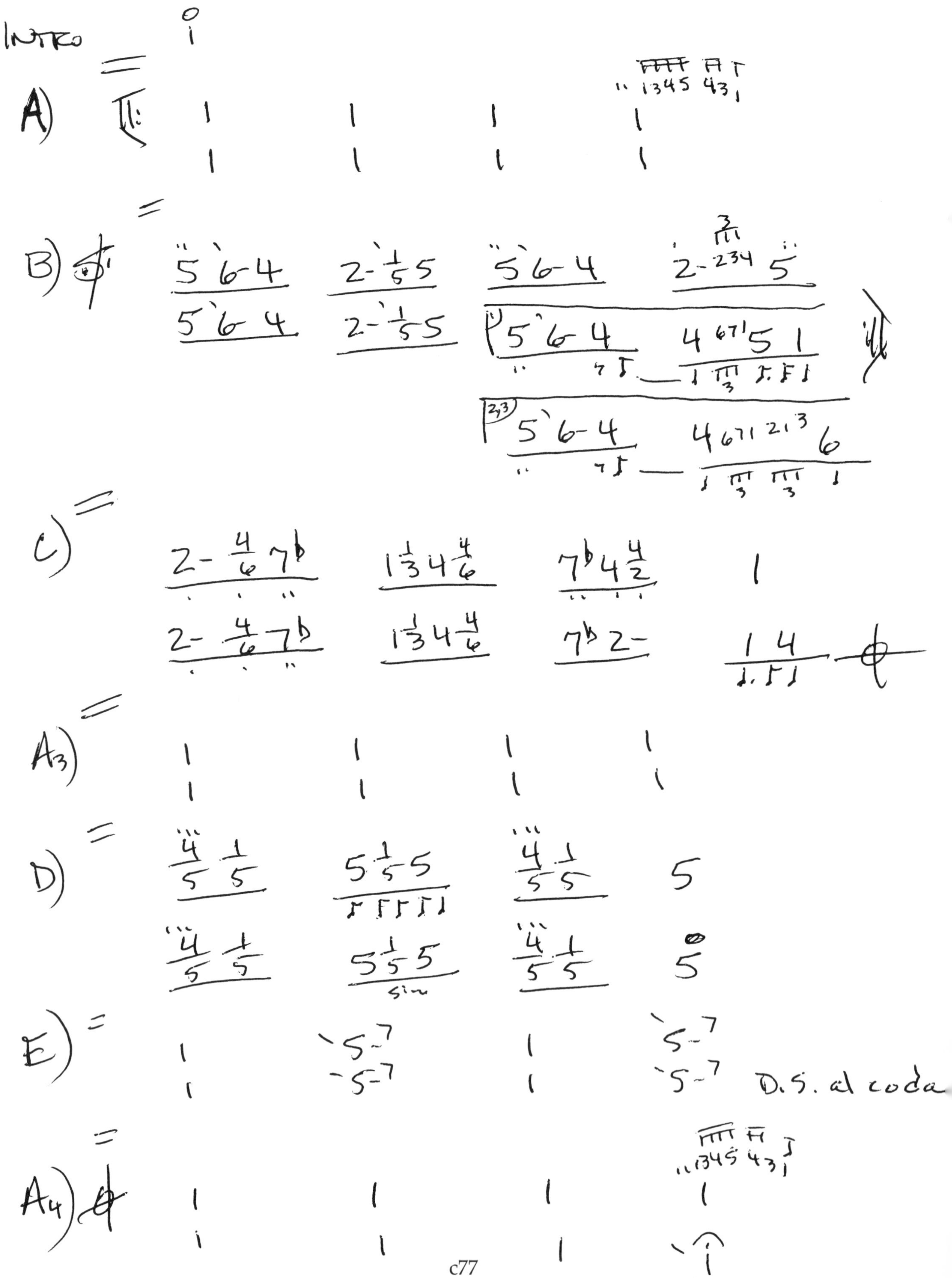

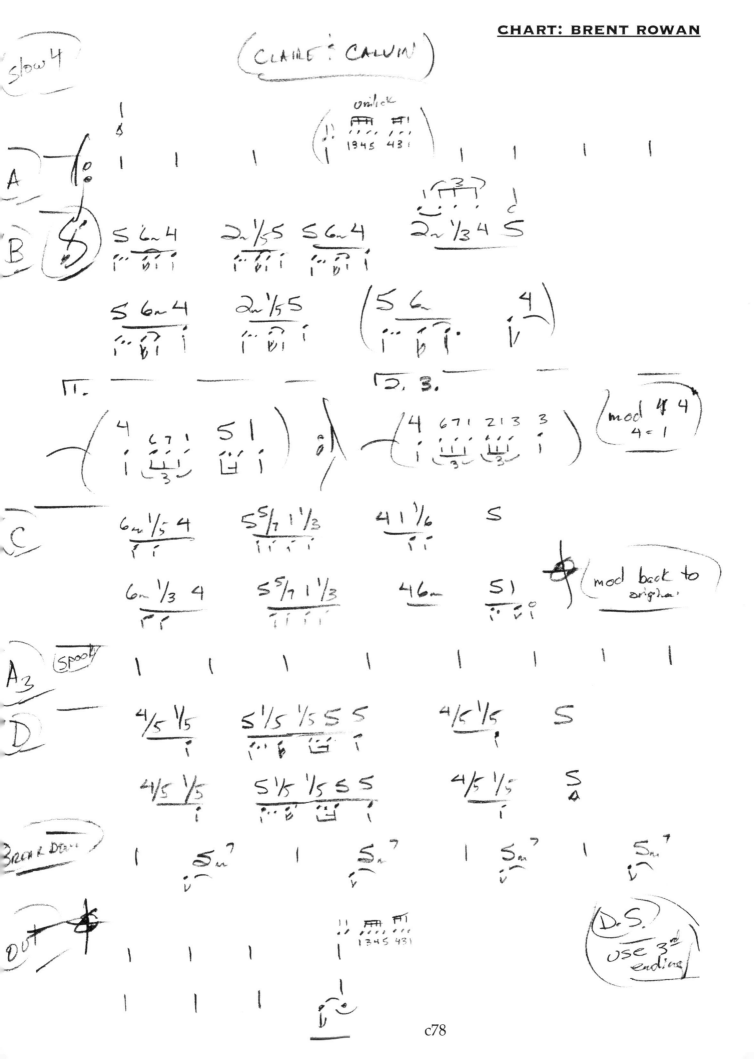

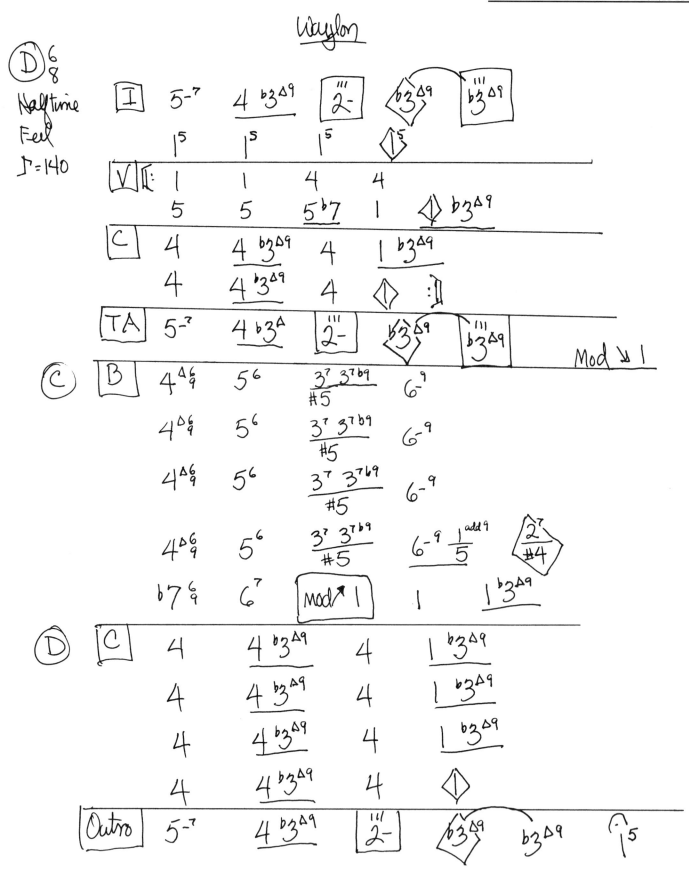

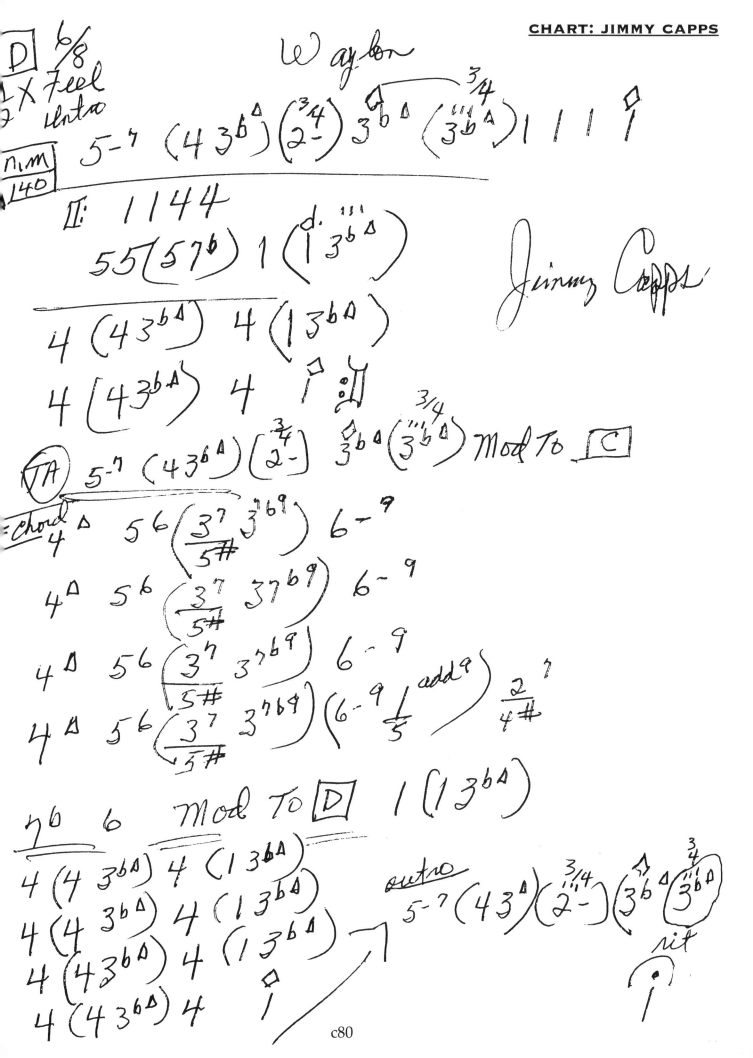

CHART: BIFF WATSON

WAYLON

6/8

INTRO	5-7 ||| 43b∆9 ||| (2-)	d. 3b∆9 (3b∆9)
	‖: 1 (NO 3RD)	1 sim	1 sim	◊ sim
V) ‖: 1 / 5	1 / 5	4 / 57b	4 / 1 1 3b
CH) 4 / 4	43b / 43b	4 / 4	1 3b / ◊
A) 5-7	43b	(2-)	d. 3b∆9 (3b∆9)
BRIDGE) 3b 6/9	4 6	27/4#	5-9
3b 6/9	4 6	27/4#	5-9
3b 6/9	4 6	27/4#	5-9
3b 6/9	4 6	27/4#	5-9 7b add 9 / 4	0/1/3
6b 6/9	57	1	1 3b∆9
CH) 4	43b	4	1 3b
4	43b	4	1 3b
4	43b	4	1 3b
4	43b	4	◊
5-7	43b∆9	(2-)	d. 3b∆9 (3b∆9) 1 (NO 3RD)

rit.

CHART: TONY HARREL

D 6/8   WAYLON

```
INTRO    5⁻⁷         4  ♭3ᵃ    (3/8) 2-   ♭3ᵃ  (3/8) ♭3
          1            1            1         1

 Vs  ‖:  1           1           4          4
          5           5          5♭7         1       1 ♭3
                                                      P.

 CH      4          4♭3          4         1♭3
         4          4♭3          4         1
                                            P.

 TA      5⁻⁷        4♭3    (3/8)2-    ♭3ᵈ       ♭3  (MOD DOWN WHOLE)
         4          5⁶         3⁷ 3♭⁹     6⁻⁹
                              #5
         4          5          3⁷         6⁻
                              #5
         4          5           3         6⁻
                              #5
         4          5           3        6⁻ 1/5   2⁷
                              #5                  #4
                                                   P.

 CH      4          4♭3         4         1♭3
         4          4♭3         4         1♭3
         4          4♭3         4         1♭3
         4          4♭3         4         1
                                           P.

OUTRO   5⁻⁷        4♭3   (3/8)2-    ♭3ᵈ    (3/8)♭3
```

CHART: EDDIE BAYERS

WAYLON

Key: D
Tempo 140
½ t~ 6/8

Intro 5-7   4/3⁶ᐞ⁹ (2-)ᴨ (3)ᐞ⁹ᴨ

R: 1   1   4   4
   5   5   5/⁶⁷   1   7/³⁶

C) 4   4/3⁶ᐞ⁹   4   1/3⁶ᐞ⁹
   4   4/3⁶ᐞ⁹   4   1:8

   4ᐞ⁶⁹   5⁶   3⁷/3⁷⁶⁹   6-⁹
                 #5
   4⁷⁶⁹   5⁶   3⁷/3⁷⁶⁹   6-⁹
                 #5
   4ᐞ⁶⁹   5⁶   3⁷/3⁷⁶⁹   6-/5⁺⁹ 2/4#

   ⁶⁷⁶⁹   6⁷ mod 1   1   1/3⁶ᐞ⁹

C) 4   4/3⁶ᐞ⁹   4   1/3⁶ᐞ⁹
   4   4/3⁶ᐞ⁹   4   1/3⁶ᐞ⁹
   4   4/3⁶ᐞ⁹   4   1/3⁶ᐞ⁹
   4   4/3⁶ᐞ⁹   4   1

OUT 5-7   4/3⁶ᐞ⁹ (2-)ᴨ   6-ᐞ⁹/3   (3ᐞ⁹)ᴨ   1⁵
                                              R..

WAYLON

CHART: CHRIS FARRE

(D) Waltz

Intro: | 5m7 | 4 3♭△9 | 2m 3♭ | ◇3♭9 |
       | 1 | 1 | 1 | |

Verse: ‖: 1 | 1 | 4 | 4 |
          5 | 5 | 5 7♭ | 1 | 1 3♭△9 |

Ch: | 4 | 4 3♭△9 | 4 | 1 3♭△9 |
    | 4 | 4 3♭△9 | 4 | ◇1 :‖

Turn: | 5m7 | 4 3♭△9 | 2m 3♭9 | ◇3♭△9 | MOD→

(C) Bridge: | 4△9 | 5⁶ | 3⁷ 3⁷♭9 / 5# | 6m7 |
            | 4△9 | 5⁶ | 3⁷ 3⁷♭9 / 5# | 6m9 |
            | 4△9 | 5⁶ | 3⁷ 3⁷♭9 / 5# | 6m9 |
            | 4△9 | 5⁶ | 3⁷ 3⁷♭9 / 5# | 6m9 1/5 | 2/4# |
            | ♭7⁹ | 6⁷ (D) MOD | 1 | 1 | 1 3♭△7 |

(D) Chorus: | 4 | 4 3♭△9 | 4 | 1 3♭△9 |
            | 4 | 4 3♭△9 | 4 | 1 3♭△7 |
            | 4 | 4 3♭△9 | 4 | 1 3♭△9 |
            | 4 | 4 3♭△9 | 4 | ◇1 |

Outro | 5m7 | 4 3♭△9 | 2m 3♭△9 | ◇3♭△9 | ◇1 |

...RITARD

CHART: CHAS WILLIAMS

Boogie Shuffle

(E) 4/4

Blues Boogie Shuffle

♩ = 103

Boogie Shuffle
CHART: CHARLIE McCo

C#

SLIDE / [5 1] [5 1] [5 1 7b / 1 1 1] 4 [4 1 3b4 5 4 3b 1 / 1 [7] [1] ⎵ ⎵ ⎵ / 3 3 3] UNISON

V| 1 5 4 4   1 5 4 4   1 5 6m 7b   [CHO] [4 1/3 2m 1]   [5 1]

[4 1/3 2m 1] [5 1] [4 1/3 2m 1] [5 1] [4 1/3 2m 1] [5 1]

[5 1 7b / 1 1 1] ø 4 [4 1 3b4 5 4 3b 1 / 1 [7] ⎵ ⎵ / 3 3 3] 1

(Br)ø 4 4 [7b 4 / ⎵3 ⎵3] 1 [7b 4 / ⎵3 ⎵3] 1 [7b 4 / ⎵3 ⎵3] [1 2]

4 4 4 [4 1 3b4 5 4 3b 1 / 1 [7] ⎵ ⎵ / 3 3 3]

V) 1 5 4 4   1 5 4 4   1 5 6m 7b   [CHO] [4 1/3 2m 1]   [5 1]

[4 1/3 2m 1] [5 1] [4 1/3 2m 1] [5 1] [4 1/3 2m 1] [5 1]

[5 1] [5 1 7b / 1 1 1] 4 [4 1 3b4 5 4 3b 1 / 1 [7] ⎵ ⎵ / 3 3 3] [5 1]

c87

CHART: TONY HARRELL

Boogie Shuffle

(E) INTRO   5̲1   5̲1   5̲1 ♭7   4   4

Vs.
   1   5   4   4
   1   5   4   4
   1   5   6⁻   ♭7

CHORUS   4⅓2-1   5̲1   4⅓2-1   5̲1
   4⅓2-1   5̲1   4⅓2-1   5̲1   5̲1 ♭7
   4 |¹. 4̲4̲1̲   ♭3̲4̲5̲   4̲♭3̲1̲ :|| |². 4

BRIDGE   ♭7̲4   1   ♭7̲4   1
   ♭7̲4   1̲2
   4   4   4   4̲4̲1̲   ♭3̲4̲5̲   4̲♭3̲1̲

Vs   1   5   4   4
   1   5   4   4
   1   5   6⁻   ♭7

CHORUS   4⅓2-1   5̲1   4⅓2-1   5̲1
   4⅓2-1   5̲1   4⅓2-1   5̲1   5̲1   5̲1 ♭7

OUTRO   4   4̲4̲1̲   ♭3̲4̲5̲   4̲♭3̲1̲   𝄆 d. 𝄇

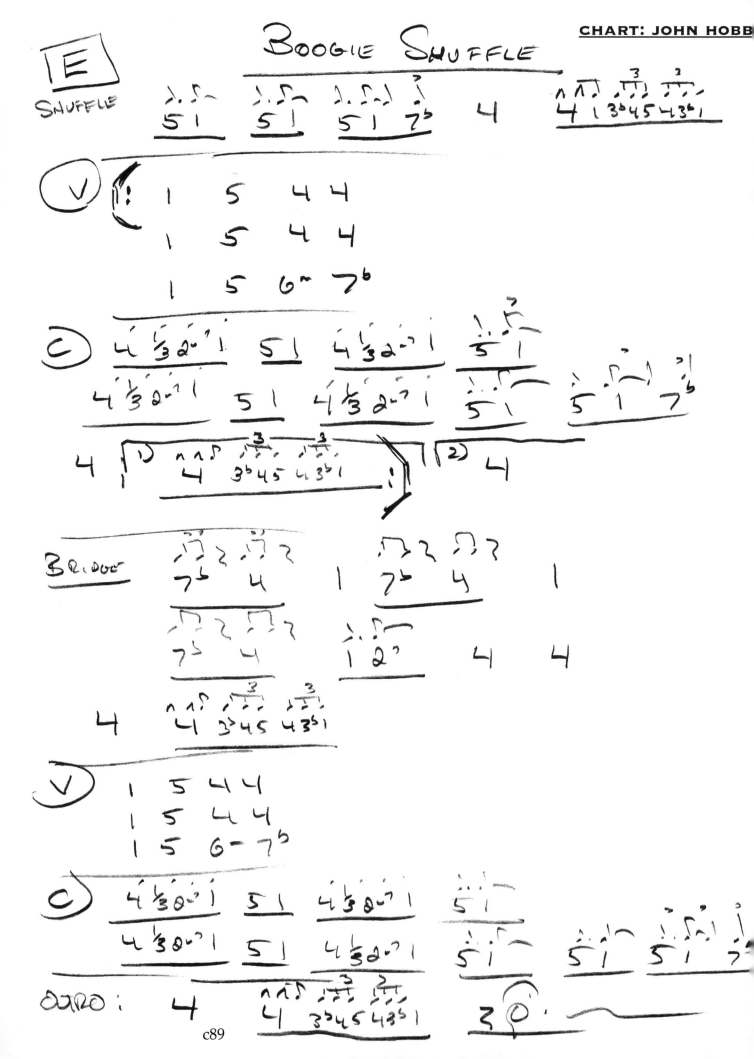

CHART: BRENT ROWAN

(103 BPM) Blues shuffle   **CHART: MIKE CHAPMA**

Boogie Shuffle

E — Guitar plays 3 pickups

Intro: | 5 1 | 5 1 | 5 1 7♭ | 4 | 4 4 1 3♭4 5 4 3♭ 1 |

Verse:
1	5	4	4
1	5	4	4
1	5	6	7♭

Chorus:
4 ½ 3 2 -1	5 1	4 ½ 3 2 -1	5 1
4 ½ 3 2 -1	5 1	4 ½ 3 2 -1	5 1
5 1 7♭	1. 4	4 4 1 3♭4 5 4 3♭ 1	:|

|2. 4 | 4 |

Bridge:
7♭ 4	1	7♭ 4	1
7♭ 4	1 2		
4	4	4	4 4 1 3♭4 5 4 3♭ 1

Verse:
1	5	4	4
1	5	4	4
1	5	6	7♭

Chorus:
| 4 ½ 3 2 -1 | 5 1 | 4 ½ 3 2 -1 | 5 1 |
| 4 ½ 3 2 -1 | 5 1 | 4 ½ 3 2 -1 | 5 1 |

Tags: | 5 1 | 5 1 7♭ |

Outro: | 4 | 4 4 1 3♭4 5 4 3♭ 1 | d. | Guitar ad libs then slam the door |

Winter Break

CHART: CHAS WILLIAMS

A/E 4/4
8th Boogie Rock
♩=145

GTR ONLY

I	1	1

V	‖: 1	1	1	5
	5	5	5	1
	1	1	1	5
	5	5	5	1

Mod ↓ to 5

E	C	54	1	54	1
		54	1	54	1 b7 :‖

Mod ↑ to Original Key

B	1 4	1 4	1 6	⟨5⟩ 4
	1 4	1 4	1 6-	5 5

GTR Only

TA	1	1

V	1	1	1	5
	5	5	5	1
	1	1	1	5
	5	5	5	1

Mod ↓ to 5

E	C	54	1	54	1
		54	1	54	1

E	C	54	1	54	1
		54	1	54	1 b7

Mod ↑ to Original Key

B	1 4	1 4	1 6-	5 4
	1 4	1 4	1 6-	5 4	↑

Chas Williams

CHART: Charlie McCoy

8ths
Elec GTR
Winter Break

V — 2 —   1115 555 1   1115 555 1

CHO [2 1] 5 [2 1] 5 [2 1] 5 [2 1] [5 4 / 1 1 / L U]

V 1115 555 1   1115 555 1

CHO [2 1] 5 [2 1] 5 [2 1] 5 [2 1] [5 4 / 1 1 / L U]

Br [1 3⁷ 4 / L U] [1 3⁷ 4 / L U] [1 6m / 1 3⁷ L U] [5 4 / 1 1 L U] [1 3⁷ 4 / L U] [1 3⁷ 4 / L U] [1 6m / 1 3⁷ L U]

5 5   Elec — 2 —

V 1115 555 1   1115 555 1

CHO [2 1] 5 [2 1] 5 [2 1] 5 [2 1] 5

CHO [2 1] 5 [2 1] 5 [2 1] 5 [2 1] [5 4 / 1 1 L U]

Br [1 4 / 1 1 L U] [1 4 / 1 1 L U] [1 6m / 1 1 L U] [5 4 / 1 1 L U] [1 4 / 1 1 L U] [1 4 / 1 1 L U] [1 6m / 1 1 L U]

[5 4 / 1 1 L U] [1̂ / 4]

CHART: JIMMY CAPPS

[A] 4/4 *Winter Break*

Intro
Elec only / /

```
||: 1  1  1  5
    5  5  5  1
    1  1  1  5
    5  5  5  1
```

(21) 5 (21) 5
(21) 5 (21)(5 d.♫ 4) :||

(d.♫ 4) (d.♫ 4) (1 6-)(5 d.♫ 4)

(d.♫ 4) (d.♫ 4) (1 6-) 5 5

GTR only short ♩ ♩

```
1  1  1  5
5  5  5  1
1  1  1  5
5  5  5  1
```

(21) 5 (21) 5
(21) 5 (21) 5
(21) 5 (21) 5
(21) 5 (21)(5 d.♫ 4)

(1 ♫ 4)(1 ♫ 4)(1 6-)(5 ♫ 4)
(1 ♫ 4)(1 ♫ 4)(1 6-)(5 ♫ 4)

Chart By
Jimmy Capps

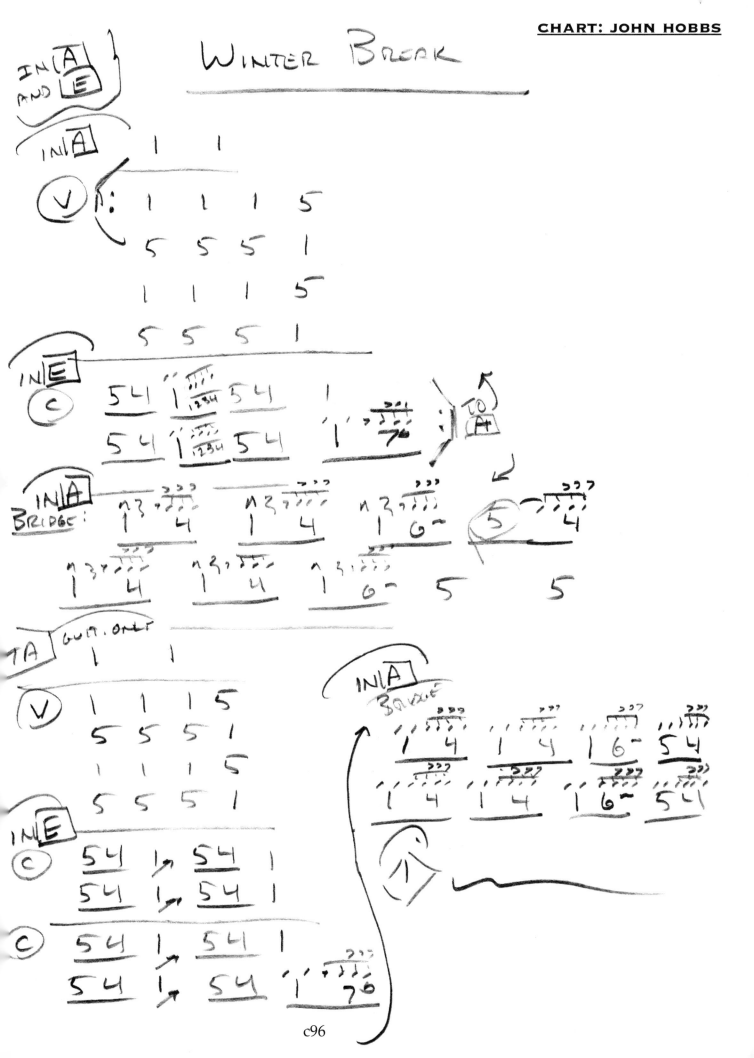

Winter Break

CHART: MIKE CHAPMA

(145 BPM) straight 8s

(A)

Intro — Guitar only...
| 1 | 1 |

Full Band → (Verse)

1	1	1	5
5	5	5	1
1	1	1	5
5	5	5	1

→ *MOD UP A FIFTH*

Chorus (E)

| 5 4 | 1 | 5 4 | 1 |
| 5 4 | 1 | 5 4 | 1. 7⁵ |

MOD BACK TO ORIGINAL KEY

Bridge (A)

| 1 4 | 1 4 | 1 6- | 5 4 |
| 1 4 | 1 4 | 1 6- | 5 | 5 |

T.A. — Guitar only...
| 1 | 1 |

Full Band → (Verse)

1	1	1	5
5	5	5	1
1	1	1	5
5	5	5	1

→ *MOD UP A FIFTH*

Chorus (E)

| 5 4 | 1 | 5 4 | 1 |
| 5 4 | 1 | 5 4 | 1. 1 |

2. | 7⁵ | *MOD BACK TO ORIGINAL KEY*

Bridge (A)

| 1 4 | 1 4 | 1 6- | 5 4 |
| 1 4 | 1 4 | 1 6- | 5 4 |

ad lib then "slam the door"

CHART: EDDIE BAYERS

Winton Brook   Key: A/E
Tempo = 145
Feel: Boogie Rock

A) (A) Guit   1   1
V)   Pi.   1   1   1   5
         5   5   5   1
         1   1   1   5
         5   5   5   1   mod to E

C) (E)   5/4   1   5/4   1   b6   } mod back to A
        5/4   1   5/4   1/7 :||

D) Br.   1/4   1/4   1/6-   5/4
       1/4   1/4   1/6-   5   5

/A   1   1
V)   1   1   1   5
    5   5   5   1
    1   1   1   5
    5   5   5   1   mod to E

(E)   5/4   1   5/4   1   1x ||: 1 :|| 2x b6
     5/4   1   5/4   1/7 mod back to A

Br.   1/4   1/4   1/6-   5/4
     1/4   1/4   1/6-   5/4   1

Pelican Shuffle

CHART: CHAS WILLIAMS

Ⓒ 4/4
2 Beat Shuffle ⓥ
4 Beat Shuffle Ⓒ
"Ray Price"
♩=100

| I | 4 3 4 #4 | [5 ♪♪] | 1 | 1 |

| V | ‖: 1 | 1 | 5 | 5 |
| | 4 | 5 | 6⁷ | 5‴/7 1 #1 |

C	2⁷	2⁷	5	5
	2⁷	2⁷	5	5‴ ♭5
	4	3⁷	6-1/5	2/#4
	4 3 4 #4	[5 ♪♪] ① 2 BEAT	1 :‖ ② 1	1‴ 7

B	[♭7⁹ ♪.♪♪♪]	♭7⁹	1	1
	[♭7⁹ ♪.♪♪♪]	♭7⁹	1 ♭7	6⁷
	2⁻⁷ 1/3 4 #4°	[5 ♪♪]	1	1 7 1 #1

C	2⁷	2⁷	5	5
	2⁷	2⁷	5	5‴ ♭5
	4	3⁷	6-1/5	2/#4
	4 3 4 #4	[5 ♪♪]	1 ♭7	6⁷

| TAG | 4 3 4 #4 | [5 ♪♪] | 1″ ♭7 7 1 | 1 𝄐 |

Chas Williams

C 4/4 Pelican Shuffle

CHART: JIMMY CAPPS

Jimmy Capps

(4 3 4 4#) (5 ♩) 1 1
_____
 4 3 4 4#

‖: 1   1   5   5
2 Beat 4   5   6 - (5̈ 1 1#)
Shuffle   7

4 Beat 2   2   5   5
Ray   2   2   5 (5̈ 4#)
Price   4   3⁷ (6 - 1/5)   2/4# 1st
Feel

(4 3 4 4#) (5 ♩) ‖: 1   1 :‖ 2nd |1 (1̈ 7)|

Tag
(4 3 4 4#) (5 ♩)

(1 7♭ 7 1) 1̂

7♭ 9th   7♭ 9th   1   1
7♭ 9th   7♭ 9th   (1 7♭) 6
(2 - 1/3 4 4#°) (5 ♩) 1 (1 7 1 1#)

2 2 5 5
2 2 5 (5̈ 4#)
4 3 (6 - 1/5) 2/4#
(4 3 4 4#) (5 ♩) (1 7♭) 6

c100

Pelican Shuffle

CHART: TONY HARREL

Ⓒ

INTRO 4 3 4 #4   5   1   1

US ‖: 1   1   5   5
     4   5   6-   5/7 1 #1

CH   2⁷   2⁷   5   5
     2⁷   2⁷   5   5 ♭5
     4   3⁷   6-1/5   2/#4

4 3 4 #4   5   1. 1   1 ‖ 2. 1   1

BR   ♭7   ♭7   1   1
     ♭7   ♭7   1 ♭7   6⁷
     2-1/3 4 #4   5   1   1 7 1 #1

CH   2⁷   2⁷   5   5
     2⁷   2⁷   5   5 ♭5
     4   3⁷   6-1/5   2/#4
     4 3 4 #4   5   1 ♭7   6

TAG 4 3 4 #4   5   1 ♭7 7 1

PELICAN SHUFFLE   CHART: CHRIS FARREN

Ⓒ

INTRO: | 4 3 4 4# / 5 / / | 1 | 1 |

VERSE: 𝄆 1 | 1 | 5 | 5 |
| 4 | 5 | 6m 5/7 | 1 1# |

CHORUS: | 2⁷ | 2⁷ | 5 | 5 |
2⁷	2⁷	5	5 5ᵇ
4	3⁷	6m 1/5	2/4#
4 3 4 4# / 5 / /	①1	1	𝄇 ② 1	1 7

[B] | ♭7⁹ | ♭7⁹ | 1 | 5 |
| ♭7⁹ | ♭7⁹ | 1 ♭7 | 6⁷ |
| 2 3 4 4# / / 5 / | 1 | 1 7 1 1# |

CHORUS: | 2⁷ | 2⁷ | 5 | 5 |
2⁷	2⁷	5	5 5ᵇ
4	3⁷	6 1/5	2/4#
4 3 4 4# / / 5 /	1 7ᵇ	6 7

TAG: | 4 3 4 4# / / 5 / | 1 7ᵇ 7 1 | ◇1 ◇

HART: EDDIE BAYERS

Pelican Shuffle   Key: C
Tempo: 100

(I) 4/3/4/4# "5"/♭   1   1

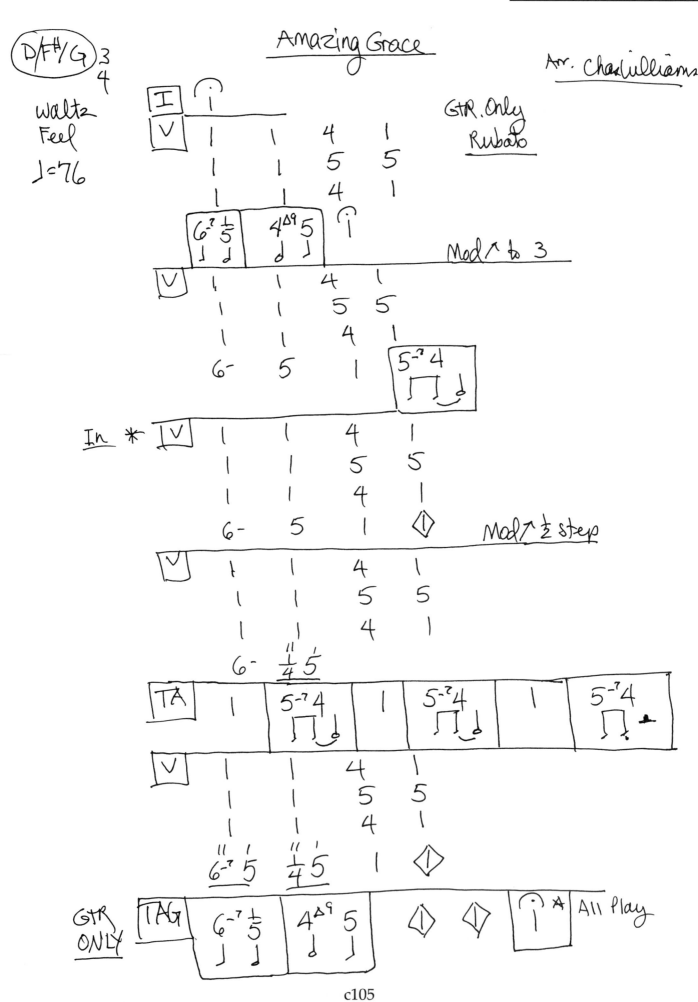

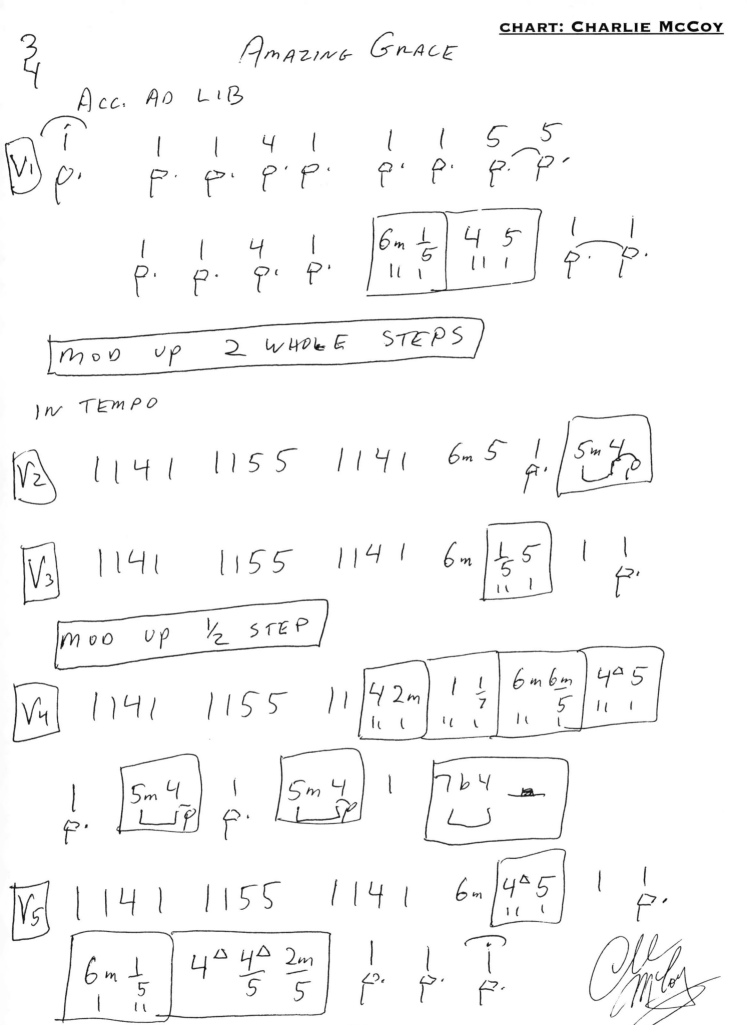

CHART: DAVID BRIGG

KEYS (D) (F#) (G)   "AMAZING GRACE"

INTRO |o.

(A) — (RUBATO)
VS
GUIT.   1 1 4 1   1 1 5 5
ONLY
         1 1 4 1 | 6m⁷/5 | 4 D9 1 5 | |o.   MOD TO
                                                (B) CHART

(B)   1 1 4 1   1 1 5 5
         1 1 4 1   6⁻ 5 1 | 5m⁷ 4 |

(C)   1 1 4 1   1 1 5 5
         1 1 4 1   6⁻ 5 1   (MOD UP 1/2)

(D)   1 1 4 1   1 1 5 5
         1 1 4 1   6⁻ | 1 5 |
                        | 4 |

TURN
   |o. 5m⁷4 | 5m⁷4 | 5m⁷4

(E)   1 1 4 1   1 1 5 5
         1 1 4 1 | 6m⁷ 5 | 1 5 | 1 1 |o.
                                4

                                              (ALL)
TAG   6⁻ 1 /5   4 b9 5   1   1   1
GUIT
ONLY   o. o. o.

CHART: JIMMY CAPPS

[D] [F#] ↑ [G]
1M] 3/4
26]

Amazing Grace

Intro ↑

| 1 1 4 1 | Gtr only
| 1 1 5 5 |
| 1 1 4 1 |
| (6- 1/5) (4∆9 1/5) | ↑ Mod to [F#]

| 1 1 4 1 |
| 1 1 5 5 |
| 1 1 4 1 |
| 6-5 1 (5- 4) |

| 1 1 4 1 |
| 1 1 5 5 |
| 1 1 4 1 |
| 6-5 1 ↑ Mod to [G]

| 1 1 4 1 |
| 1 1 5 5 |
| 1 1 4 (1 5/7) |
| 6- (1/5 5) |

TA 1(5-4) 1(5-4) 1(5-4)

| 1 1 4 1 |
| 1 1 5 5 |
| 1 1 4 1 |
| (6-5)(1/4 5) 1 ↑

Tag Gtr only

(6- 1/5)(4∆9 1/5)

↑ ↑ ↑ all Play

Jimmy Capps

c108

CHART: BIFF WATSON

AMAZING GRACE

3/4

INTRO = ⌢1
GUITAR - RUBATO

V)
1	1	4	1
1	1	5	5
1	1	4	1
6⁷¹/5	4⁹⌢5	⌢1 (MOD UP MAJOR 3RD)

V) = DOBRO
1	1	4	1
1	1	5	5
1	1	4	1
6-	5	1	5-4 / ♩♩♩

V) =
1	1	4	1
1	1	5	5
1	1	4	1 ♩
6-	5	1	⌢1 (MOD UP ½ STEP)

V) =
1	1	4	1
1	1	5	5
1	1	4	1
6-	1/4 5		

TA) =
| 1 | 5-4 / ♩♩♩ | 1 | 5-4 / ♩♩♩ | 1 | 5-4 / ♩♩ |

V) =
1	1	4	1
1	1	5	5
1	1	4	1 ♩.
6⁷-5	1/4 5	1	♩.
6⁷¹/5	4⁹⌢5	♩.	♩.	⌢1

c110

Charlie McCoy

Charlie studied music at the University of Miami. He moved to Nashville and began working recording sessions in the early '60's. After playing on Roy Orbison's hit, *Candy Man*, Charlie built up to more than 400 sessions a year. In addition to sessions with country artists, Charlie has played on many of Elvis Presley's records, as well as three albums for Bob Dylan. Charlie also played harmonica and served as the musical director for the Hee Haw television show for 18 years. He arranged and wrote all the charts that the band read. Charlie has had quite a recording career of his own, with 29 albums as an artist. For information on how to order Charlie's records and learn more about his amazing career, visit his web site: www.charliemccoy.com.

Charlie said that in 1960, none of the session musicians used charts. They memorized songs, then recorded. Charlie noticed Neal Matthews using numbers to map out multiple songs for *The Jordanaires*. McCoy adapted Neal's numbering system into rhythm section chord charts. Ray Edenton, Bob Moore, Pete Wade, Weldon Myrick, Harold Bradley, David Briggs, and Wayne Moss were some of the musicians playing on most of the Nashville records in the early 60's. They all say that Charlie McCoy was the first one to pick up the number system from Neal Matthews. Bob Moore said that on most sessions in the early 60's, players memorized the songs and didn't even use charts.

Ray Edenton said,"Neal Matthews used the number system with the group (Jordanaires), but we never picked up on it at all until Charlie came here. He's the one, as far as I'm concerned, who brought the number system here. Neal wrote numbers for the singers, but it wasn't nearly as complicated as what Charlie brought here."

As well, Pete Wade said Charlie McCoy and Larry Butler were the 2 guys that taught him the number system.

Charlie writes his charts horizontally across the page in groups of four measures; sometimes 16 bars on one line, like on *String Of Pearls*. He draws a box around split bars and writes diamonds beneath the chord number. For rhythmic notation like on *Winter Break*, Charlie writes the rhythms beneath the chord changes. Look at the 2nd Bridge in the example below and see how he writes the rhythm. The 8th notes are grouped under the chord they go with and there is a long beam from the first chord to the pushed second chord. This beaming gives you a visual feel for the timing between the chords.

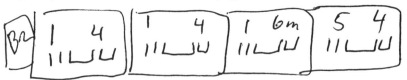

Also, look at how Charlie writes pushes on *Boogie Shuffle*. He places an arrow before a simple pushed bar, but writes out rhythm for a more complex rhythm.

David Briggs

David Briggs played keys in the original rhythm section at Rick Hall's Fame Studio, in Muscle Shoals. He was in the rhythm section on hit songs by Arthur Alexander, Jimmy Hughes, Tommy Roe and The Tams.

David moved to Nashville in 1964 as an artist and songwriter for Decca Records. On an Elvis session in 1965, Floyd Cramer was late and David got called to come play on the record. *Love Letters* and *How Great Thou Art* were the first of many songs he recorded with Elvis over a period of 11 years. He then went on the road with him in '76, a year before Elvis died.

In the late 60's David started Quadrafonic Sound, where Margaritaville was recorded. He also played on Drift Away at Quad, which was written by Mentor Williams. David wrote many string arrangements for Williams' productions, in Europe and the U.S., including artist Kim Carnes. In 1976, David opened his studio, House Of David. His first client there was Joe

Cocker. David has played on hits by many country artists, including: Dolly Parton, Waylon Jennings and Roy Orbison, but he calls himself an "Island of Pop" in Nashville because most of his hits have been pop records. He has played on records by George Harrison, Eric Clapton, Neil Young and Bob Seger.

Larry Paxton, bassist for the Opry staff band, says he is a fan of David Briggs chart writing. David said he likes to write $\flat 7$ instead of $7\flat$ because he's written so many string arrangements, where in traditional notation, the sharp or flat sign goes in front of the note. David underlines evenly split bars. However, he has a unique way of writing syncopated measures with sort of a bucket instead of a complete box around the bar. Also, look at *Uncle John's Cabin*, where David uses a double Sign and double Coda in the A section for the second D.S.

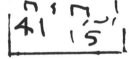

Lura Foster

Lura moved to Nashville in 1979 after studying piano and voice for four years at Austin Peay University. Once in Nashville, Lura began working on television shows, *Nashville On the Road* and *Pop Goes The Country*. While with these shows, she learned about the *Nashville Number System* from band leader, Jerry Whitehurst. She combined her knowledge of formal music notation with the basic number system to concoct her own method of translating music to paper.

In 1983, Jerry hired Lura to write all the charts for the show, *Nashville Now*. *Nashville Now* was replaceed by *Music City Tonight* and then *Prime Time Country*. "Lura Foster writes the best charts in town", Jerry says. So, since '83, Lura was responsible for all the

music that was read and played by the *Nashville Now* band and later versions of the variety show. I asked Charlie McCoy who's charts he liked. Without hesitation, he said," Lura Foster". Lura says, "It's too bad that some people still scoff at the *Nashville Number System* of writing charts, and think its too simplified." However, her charts are like a complete score, since she is writing arrangments for a very large band on one piece of paper.

Lura has devised a few of her own chart writing techniques. For instance, instead of using slashes or parentheses for split bars, she boxes in measures that have more than one chord. The box emphasizes that you are looking at only one measure, and allows room above the chords for rhythmic notation if there is any syncopation. If there is just a straight rhythm, she notates the beats with dots over the chord changes.

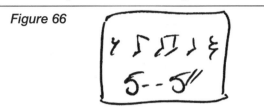

Figure 66

The double slash after a chord (Fig.66) means to hit the chord and cut it off. Also, Lura prefers to write out rhythmic figures rather than use push signs.

Another sign Lura uses is an arrow above a melody note pointing up or down to show whether to play the note in a higher or lower octave. Figure 67 is Lura's chart for the first verse of *String Of*

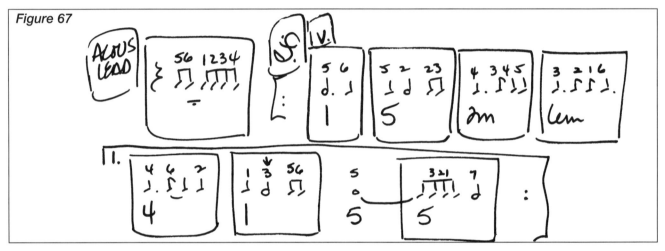

Pearls, with the melody written above the chord changes.

One more example of Lura's use of formal notational symbols is she uses a one measure repeat sign ✕ to indicate that the previous measure is repeated and played exactly as before.

Figure 68

Look at *White Hardware*. Bar 3 of the verse has the same sign, but doubled in order to play the two previous measures instead of one. So, Fig. 68 is a total of 6 bars.

Another interesting detail of Lura's charting is how she writes out the bass notes when they alternate. Check figure 69 in the verse of the song, Waylon. Lura also has created special chart

paper that she uses with staff lines at the top and bottom of the page. Those are so she or the player can write out a melody notation using standard notation.

Brent Rowan

Brent got his first electric guitar when he was 11, but taught himself how to read music in high school with hopes of playing trumpet in the U.S.Navy Band. Instead, he moved to Nashville. After some time doing low paying road work in a gospel trio, Brent got a break in the studio and was hired to play on John Conlee's record, "Friday Night Blues". He's played on every Conlee record since. Brent has worked on over 10,000 recording sessions, which equals over 100,000,000 records sold. He's played on records by George Strait, Shania Twain, Sting, Brian Wilson, Randy Travis, Neil Diamond, Olivia Newton-John, Lynyrd Skynyrd, and Alabama, to name a few.

In addition to playing, Brent has produced all of Joe Nichols records, which includes the single, "What's A Guy Got To Do To Get A Girl In This Town". (That's Brent's guitar solo.) He also produced the successful debut cd by Julie Roberts.

Brent says he writes really detailed charts when he's producing. His charts are written to the note becuse he's arranged the song before he gets to the studio and that organization saves him a song per record. If there's a $250,000 budget for 10 songs, that's the kind of savings people will notice. If there's a band unison lick, he'll write that out so the instrumentalist won't have to spend time trying to figure out the passage by ear:

Look at one of Brent's split bars: 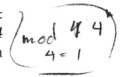 This is a bar of "Four, Split One Over Three."

The "One Over Three" is written with a diagonal slash. Also, notice Brent's modulation instructions in Claire & Calvin: He says "**Mod up to 4**", but also that, "**4 = 1**". In other words, the *4 chord* is now the new *1 chord*. One more thing, Brent, like John Hobbs, puts a slash through the stem of a 7 or 9 to mean Major seventh or ninth: ⁊

Biff Watson

The day after Biff Watson graduated from high school in 1971, he packed up his clock radio, a pillow and his guitar and hitch-hiked to Nashville. He played on the road with Tracy Nelson and Crystal Gayle for a couple of years before he was doing enough session work to stay in town and make a living.

Biff is still one of the first to call acoustic guitarists in Nashville. Once, on a Shania Twain session, Mutt Lang, Shania's husband and producer, asked "Who wants to do the charts?" Everyone in the session band pointed to Biff. Biff said Mutt would bring songs with detailed demo recordings and have very explicit instructions about what to play. I asked Biff what are the circumstances for most of the sessions where you write charts? He said that about one out of ten producers brings in a chart. "A lot of the time, the producer or songwriter will play the song for everybody on an acoustic and the players will write a chart. 90% of Toby Keith sessions are charted this way," he said.

The first thing I noticed about Biff's charts is, he uses what looks like a backwards apostrophe to signal a push. Here's a bar from Claire & Calvin (figure 70). In this bar, the **6-** is pushed.

Also, notice where Biff writes rhythmic notation; beneath the underlined split bar. Figure 71 is from Perfume and Bubblegum.

Look at Biff's chart of Waylon. In the intro, bar 6, he writes "(no 3rd)" to show the **1** chord has no 3rd. On bars 7, 8 and 9, he writes,"sim", by the chord, which means, "similar"; play the same chord voicing as the previous bar (with no 3rd. Also, in the song, Waylon, **3/8** bars (half bars) are notated with parentheses and no other marking.

One more thing, look at Biff's melodic notation. The notes rise and fall with the direction of the melody.

Jimmy Capps

Jimmy moved to Nashville in 1958, while working with the Louvin Brothers. He played on the *Grand Ole Opry* for the first time in 1962. In 1968, Jimmy became a full time guitarist for the Opry staff band, and has played Friday and Saturday nights there even though the band has changed personnel.

As well, Jimmy has played on a lot of great records. A few of the classic songs that he played guitar on are *Stand By Your Man*, by Tammy Wynette, *Easy Lovin*, by Freddy Hart, *The Gambler* and *Coward Of The County*, by Kenny Rogers, and *Elvira*, by the Oak Ridge Boys.

Jimmy learned the *Nashville Number System* on his own from recording sessions and working on television. He humbly says, "My charts may not be musically correct but everybody has their own style of writing them." Jimmy writes a good portion of the charts read by the Grand Ole Opry staff band. His charts correctly contain all the information needed to help the band sound great every night.

Jimmy puts all split bars in parentheses. Odd length measures are also shown in parentheses and have the appropriate time signatures over them. For measures where the chord is held, Jimmy uses small diamonds over the chord and ties to any measure where the diamond is held more than 1 bar.

Eddie Bayers

Eddie Bayers is from Peutaxant, Maryland. He studied classical piano beginning at age 7 and continued to study classical and jazz music at Laney College and later at the University of California at Berkeley.

In 1973, Eddie moved to Nashville and worked for about two years as a keyboard player. At age 24, he was playing keys on a gig in Nashville's Printer's Alley with Larrie Londin. Eddie says, during that gig, Larrie inspired him to switch over to drums as his main instrument.

This was early in a huge career in which Eddie has recorded with an endless list of major artists including Alan Jackson, Bob Seger, John Fogerty, Suzy Boguss, Tricia Yearwood, The Judds, and Wynonna. A few career stats earned by Eddie Bayers: Won *Academy of Country Music* Drummer of the year for '92 and '93; *Music Row's* #1 drummer; *Modern Drummer* Magazine's #1 Country Drummer for '93; 3 CMA Awards for playing on the single of the year, and one Musician of the Year Nomination.

When Eddie moved to Nashville he had never worked with the *Nashville Number System.* However, from classical studies, he knew about the use of Roman numerals and figured bass. The first Nashville charts Eddie experienced didn't utilize formal music notation. Then he saw Dennis Burnside write rhythm charts using numbers combined with formal notation.

Other stylistic differences he noticed were the different kinds of split bar notations and signs for pushes and 2/4 bars. Look at Eddie's charts and notice his evenly split bars are divided with a diagonal slash. However, his other split bars are in parentheses and many have notation to show rhythmic changes. Also, Eddie uses x's over rhythm notes to show stops.

Eddie says "It was interesting to watch how everybody dealt with their own ways of using the Nashville system. As I got into more sessions, the leaders of the sessions or the producer passed out your chart and you'd see little things. Then it's a matter of inquiring, "What's this?"

"The Number System is so valid. There really isn't any other form to me as far as basic recording or even learning a song. Once you learn the system, it makes total sense. Especially in a transposition situation."

Eddie said, "It's funny how people get biased. I remember working with Mike Post who had everything notated out when you worked for him. When working out certain modulations he always made the joke, "Let's see them write this out in numbers." "The thing was," Eddie says, "it can be written out in numbers, easy. Basically by using the English language, like: 'Mod to the b3, or the *1* equals the *4*, or whatever. I've never seen the number system not being able to be used."

Eddie used number charts on the '93 Bob Seger album, *Fire Inside,* and John Fogerty's '93 album; a couple more examples of non Nashville type sessions.

For drummers new to Nashville, Eddie suggests, "Try to learn charts that others are using. Find your own method until you are able to start realizing how to utilize what everybody else is doing." Eddie used to watch Larrie Londin years ago write a chart full of *1*'s to represent chord changes, then notate accents accordingly. "If the job gets done, to me that's the bottom line; however you can get to the situation of learning a song as quick as possible and being able to play it."

John Hobbs

John grew up between L.A. and Bakersfield, California. He already had a fine music education in high school and was adept at reading, writing and arranging music before attending college at Longbeach State. After one year of college, John quit to go on the road with Kenny Rogers and the First Edition. In 1970, while doing his first demo recordings, John says his good friend, steel guitarist, Jay Dee Maness, taught him the Nashville Number System and how to play country piano. ("the left hand plays with the bass and the right hand plays with the rhythm guitar.") Around '85, John began doing a lot of country sessions in L.A. with artists produced by Jimmy Bowen. He says, "Jimmy didn't use number charts, but had arrangers write out music for the players. These were *two line master rhythm charts* with treble clef and bass clef (used to write out any guitar lines and bass lines), then the chord symbol in the middle." John began commuting to do Nashville session work and moved to Nashville in 1994. He played on George Strait's, "Does Fort Worth Ever Cross Your Mind"(The Chair), LeeAnn Rimes', "Blue", Shania Twain's, "Come On Over" and records from Doug Dillard to B.B.King.

John says that, "When working with numbers and traditional notation, one makes the other better. The number system helps you think of the relativity of the changes instead of just the chord." So, it's no surprise to find rhythmic notation to show exactly what's going on in John's charts. Notice in the split bar, the small forward arrow over some notes. John uses the arrow in it's traditional manner to show the note is accented. Also, John uses a **7** with a line through the stem as a major seventh. He says this is an old jazz notation short cut.

Chris Farren

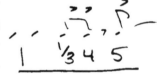

Chris majored in English with a minor in Music at East Carolina University. He moved from LA to Nashville in 1998. Chris has produced and/or written over 100 songs for film and tv, including *We Were Soldiers*, with Mel Gibson and *My Cousin Vinny*. Even though Chris has produced records for Olivia Newton-John, Boy Howdy, Pam Tilllis, Kevin Sharp and the Warren Brothers, his biggest record was Deana Carter's Strawberry Wine, which sold over 5 million copies.

Chris says he produced sessions in Nashville a couple of years before he felt comfortable writing his own number charts for guys in the studio. He says session keyboardist, John Hobbs, showed him the fine points of the system. Notice Chris' push sign on the *4 over 6* chord from Amazing Grace. Chris also has a good use of rhythmic notation. Here's a bar from the chorus of Perfume & Bubblegum. See how he writes rhythms through the split bar underline.

117

Tony Harrell

Tony moved to Nashville in 1984 after majoring in Piano Performance and Mechanical Engineering at SMU. His first 3 years in Nashville were spent on the road with Johhny Paycheck and Mel McDaniel. Tony has since stayed in town and played on records from Randy Travis, Hank Jr., Keith Urban and Rodney Crowell, to Peter Cetera, Michael Bolton, India Arie and Andy Griffith.

Tony says he first learned about the number system from guitarist, Danny Parks, whom he shared a house with during their early years in Nashville. Look at one of Tony's split bars from the chorus of Perfume & Bubblegum. Notice how he puts notation beneath the split bar-line and only notates the 2nd half of the bar where there is a different rhythm.

For a song in a minor key, Tony said he doesn't automatically use a **6 minor** as the **1 chord**. "You have to find your comfort zone for the tonal center", he said. "If a song starts on **1 minor** and ends on **1 minor,** I'll chart it as a minor key." Look at Tony's charts and see why he's the one most often writing the charts at a session.

Mike Chapman

Mike is from Athens, Alabama. He learned to read music for Band in High school and took some theory courses while at Athens College. During college Mike was playing bass in Huntsville clubs. The singer recorded demos in Nashville and would sometimes bring back number charts from the sessions to show the band.

By 1979 Mike was playing on demos in Muscle Shoals and had a good understanding of the number system since they had been using it there for years. Songwriters started bringing Mike to Nashville to play on their demos, so when he decided to move to Nashville in 1984, he already had done a lot of sessions in town. In 1988, He got a call to play bass on the first Garth Brooks record, which included,"If Tomorrow Never Comes" and "The Dance". Mike also played on all Garth's cd's except "Chris Gaines". He has also played on #1 records by LeAnn Rimes, Joe Diffie, Kathy Mattea, Sammy Kershaw and BlackHawk.

The first thing I notice about Mike's charts is where he circles 2/4 bars, underlines and puts 2 quarter notes above. Also, look at Mike's check mark, push sign. To be clear, Mike writes out the word when there is a "stop". At the end of *Boogie Shuffle*, "Slam The Door", refers to the band, cued by drums, to hit a short, sharp attack, ending note, meaning the song is over.

Chas Williams

I am a guitarist/dobroist and moved to Nashville in 1979 after a couple of semesters at Berklee College of Music. I picked up bits and pieces of the *Nashville Number System* while working in writer's nights bands and doing demo sessions. I combined number system ideas with formal notation I had learned. I soon realized that this was how it was done anyway. At writer's nights, the band backed 20 to 30 songwriters per night. We played their original songs with no rehearsal, just number charts. We wrote most of the charts ourselves and received great ear training taking dictation from thousands of song demos.

I've sort of combined chart writing techniques from several musicians. I like to underline split bars and box in 2/4 measures and bars that need rhythmic notation. Splitting this way helps a chart look clean. A diagonal slash to divide a split bar, eg. 4/5, looks a lot like a chord with a different bass note. In addition to the slash, parentheses take up a lot of space and can clutter up a chart if there are a lot of split bars.

When rhythmic notation is needed, I've started putting it below the chord, because sometimes, you don't know when to leave space above; especially if you're charting a song you've never heard.

I like to use diamonds, but sometimes, just a whole note works well. I also like the mute sign: $\overset{\blacktriangle}{5}$ but Paul Scholten at County Q uses what they call a *Dorito* around the chord to signal a clean stop.

More Charts

This chapter of the book is a collection of charts handwritten by 17 musicians who are playing or producing sessions everyday and really influencing the music that is made in Nashville. These players were kind enough to send me charts they had written. Some of the charts are from a gig or session, some were written for other players to read and some were just written for the player's own use, with no intention of anyone else ever seeing the chart...

Some of these players, like Dann Huff, you may have heard of from producing Keith Urban and LeAnn Rimes, but you may not have heard of Jeff King, who's played guitar on records by Reba McIntyre, Phil Vassar and Randy Travis, or Reese Wynans, who played keys on Stevie Ray Vaughn's records and is working as a studio musician here in Nashville. Search these names on www.allmusic.com and see which of your favorite records these musicians have played on.

- **Harold Bradley**-Studio Bassist and Tic-Tac Bass
- **Dann Huff**-Studio Guitarist/Producer
- **Barry Beckett**-Studio Keyboardist/Producer
- **Bob Patin**-Studio Keyboardist
- **Jim Brown**-Studio Keyboardist/Guitarist
- **Brent Mason**-Studio Guitarist
- **Randy Scruggs**-Studio Guitarist/Producer
- **Danny Parks**-Studio Guitarist
- **Paul Scholten**-Studio Drummer/Owner: County Q Studio
- **Dave Pomeroy**-Studio Bassist
- **Troy Lancaster**-Studio Guitarist
- **Reese Wynans**-Studio Keyboardist/Stevie Ray Vaughn
- **Andy Most**-Studio Guitarist/Producer
- **Larry Paxton**-Studio Bassist/Opry Staff Band
- **Kerry Marx**-Studio Guitarist/Opry Staff Band
- **Jeff King**-Studio Guitarist
- **Jim Hoke**-Studio Sax & Horn player/Arranger

CHART: HAROLD BRADLEY

F to F#

INTRO - COUNT 1 2 3 4 (1 6mi) (1 6mi) VOICES + PIANO

Ⓐ (1 5) 1 4 4 (1 6mi) (1 5) 1
       PIANO

Ⓐ1 (1 5) 1 4 4 (1 6mi) (1 5) 1
        PIANO

Ⓑ 4 4 2 2 5 rit.
   VOICES 4/4

Ⓐ2 (1 5) 1 4 4 (1 6mi) (1 5) 1
        PIANO

Ⓑ2 4 4 2 2 5 rit.
    VOICES 2/4

Ⓐ3 (1 5) 1 4 4 (1 6mi) (1 5) (1 5) 1 0
        PIANO   TEMPO   PIANO FILL

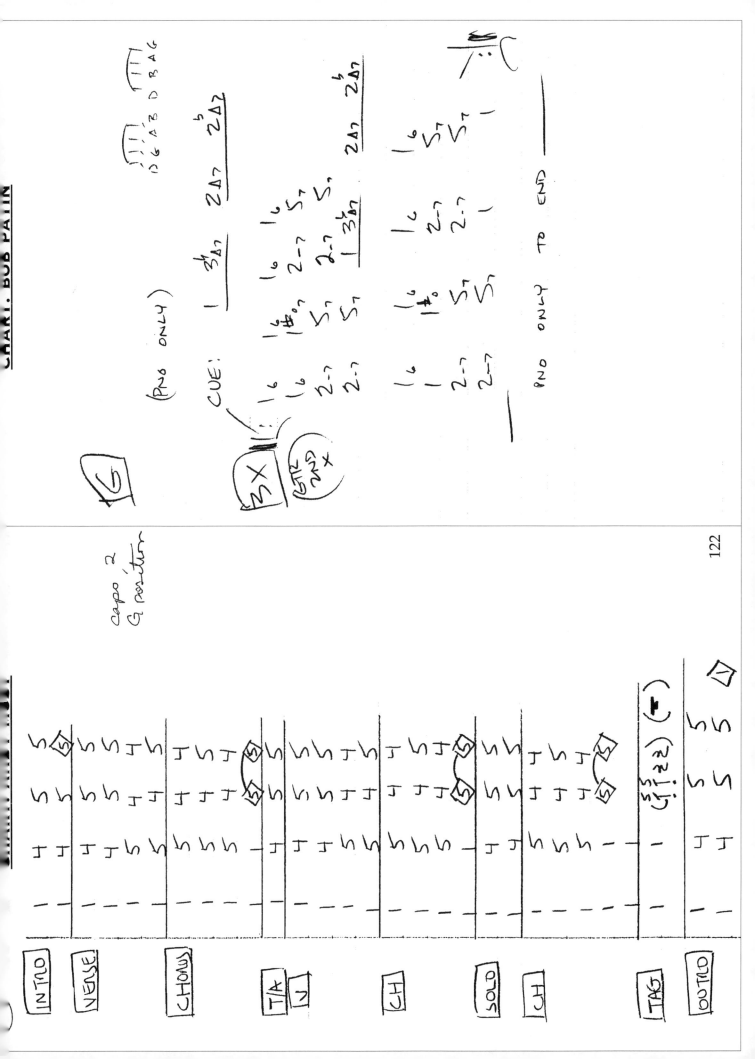

CHART: BARRY BECKETT

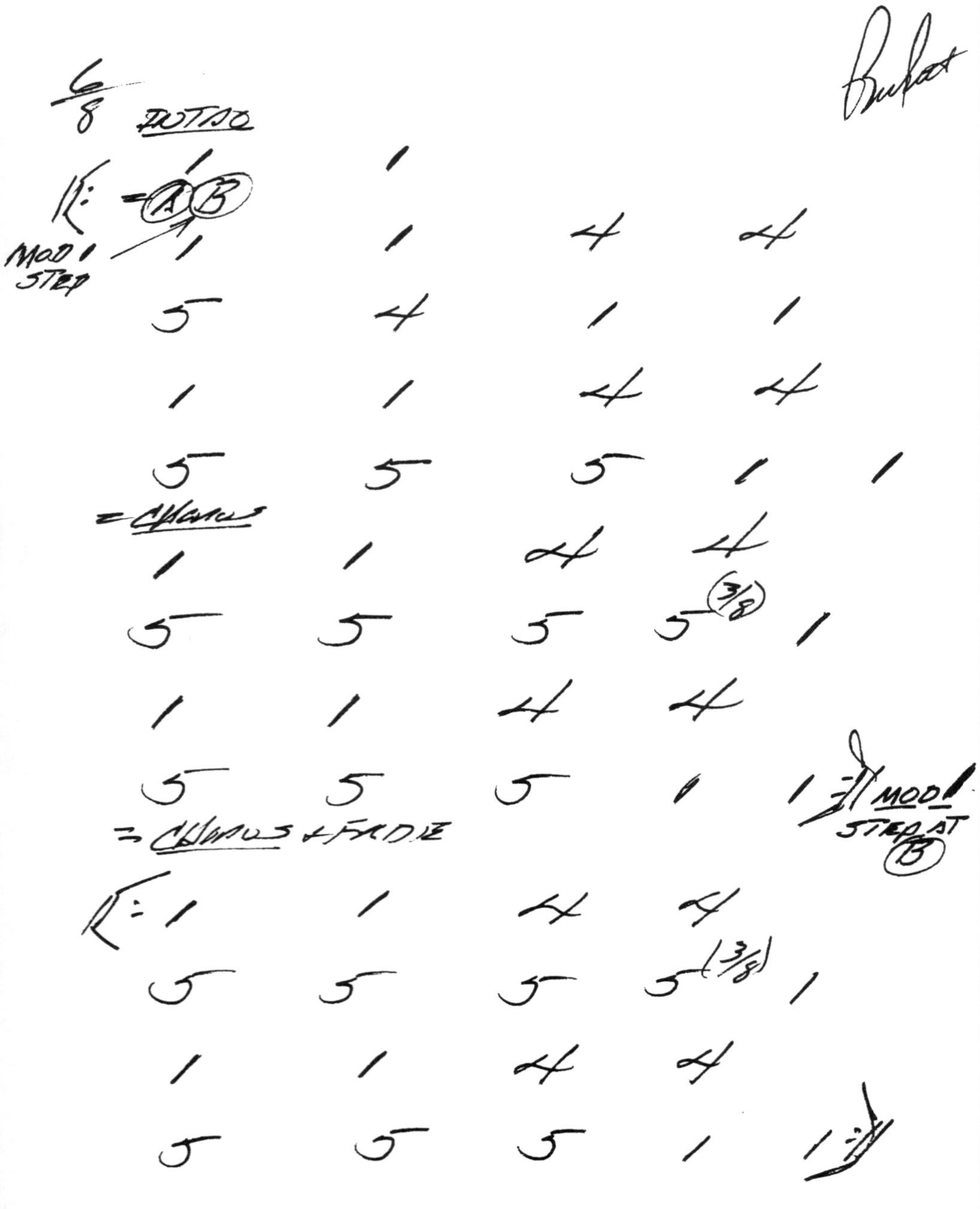

CHART: DANN HUFF

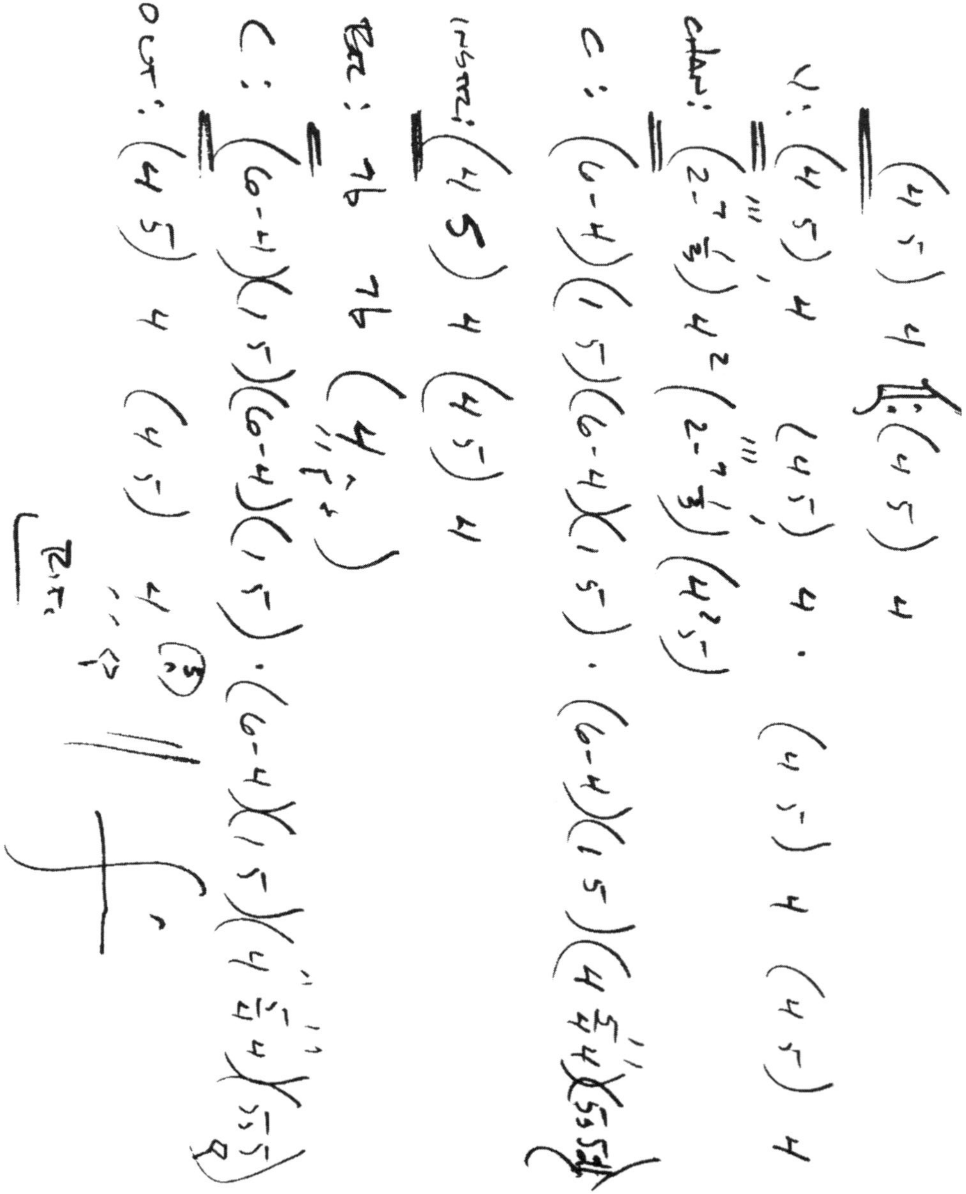

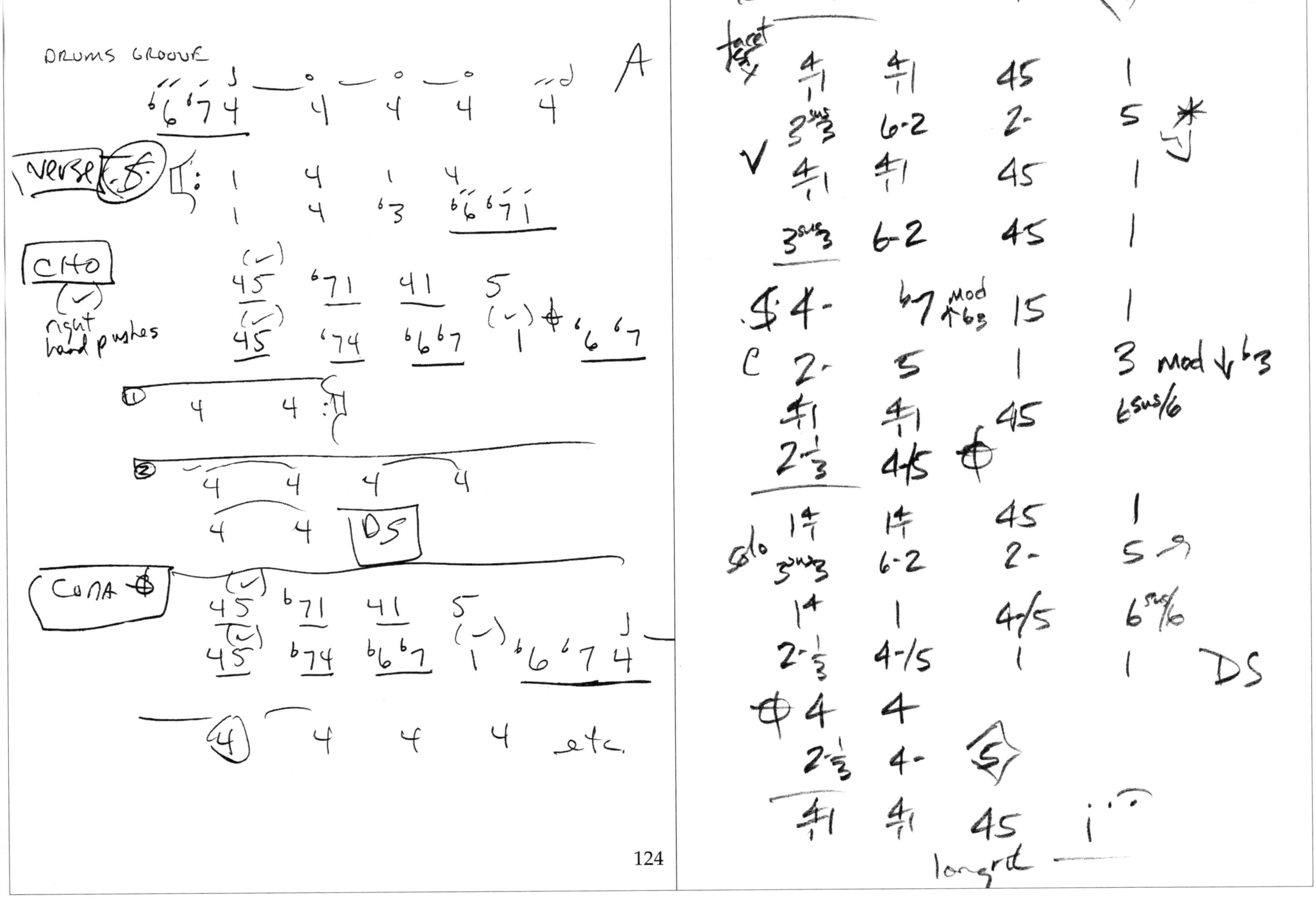
DRUMS GROOVE
A
Verse
CHO
right hand pushes
DS
CODA
etc.
E/G
facet
C
solo
long rit

CHART: JIM BROWN

Jim "Moose" Brown

| 1 4 5 1 |

V | - 5 1 - 5 1 ² - 1 5 6⁻ 5 1 ⁷
  r.uf3
  — 5
  4 1 - 4 1 - 5

Ch | - 1 4 5 1 - 1 4 5 1

[Solo]

Bridge 6⁻ 4 2⁻5 1 - 6⁻ 4 ◇5⁻ ◇5⁻ ◇5⁻
                        stop 1x
                        only   D.C.
                        F♯ — 5

Ch 5/♯4◇ 4 5 1 - 1 4 5 1 - 1 4 5
Ch — 4 5 1 - 1 4.5 5 5 5
                              F♯ —
| . 1 4 5 1 - 1 4 5 1 :|| Fade

CHART: JIM HOKE

C

INTRO: | 1 b4 4 — 1 b4 4 — | Fdl

Fiddle | — 5 4 4 | — 5 5 5 | Fdl
       | — b4 4 5 | — 5 4 — | Sindc

       | — 5 b4 4 | HARP
                     F♯×3

Dobro | 5 5 5 5 | 4 4 4 4
       | 5 5 5 5 | 5 4 4 5

Ch: | — 1 4 5 1 | — 1 4 5 —

       | — 5 b4 4 | — 4 4 4 | Dobro

Dobro | 5 5 5 5 | 4 4 4 4
       | 5 5 5 5 | 4 4 5 5

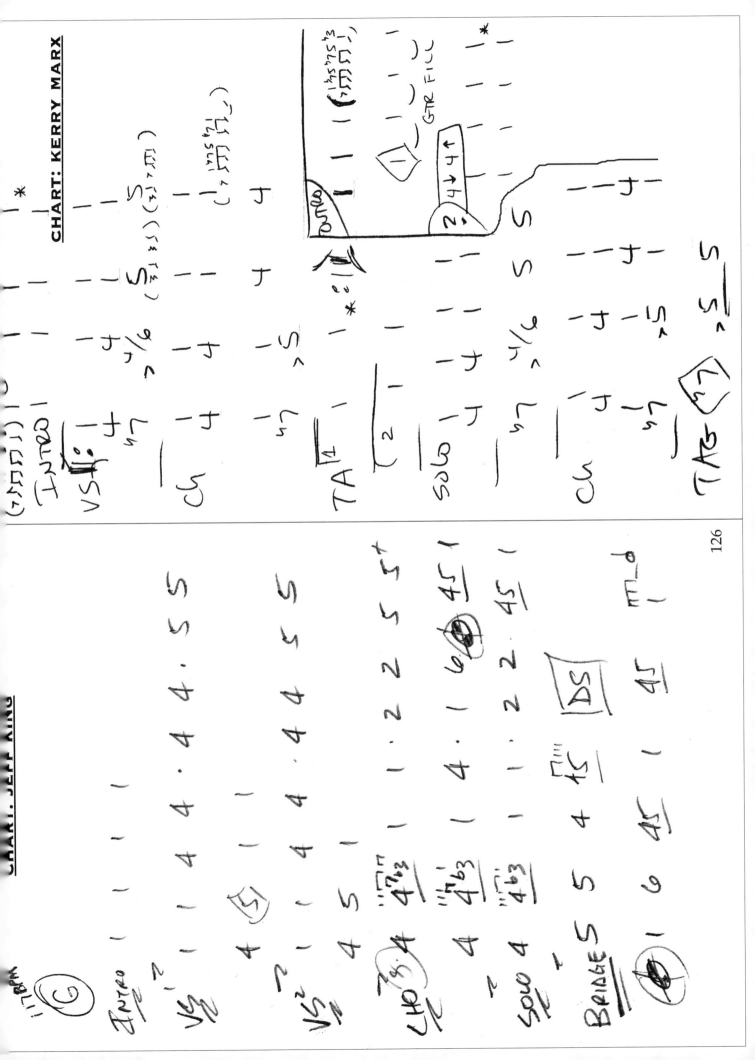

CHART: RANDY SCRUGGS

R. Scruggs

(G) 4/4 or

(INTRO) 1 | 1/7 6- 6-/5 | 4 3 | 5⁻ˢᵘˢ 5 |

(V1) 1 | 5 | 4 | 6- | 1 1/6-5 |
     4 | 4 | 6- | 5 1 |
     1 | 5 | 4 | 6- | 1 1/6-5 |
     — | 1 | — | 6- | 5 1 1/6-5 |

(V2,3) 𝄆 1 | 1/7 6 6/5 | 4 5/5 | 4 3 | 5⁻ˢᵘˢ 5 𝄇 D.S.

C H⁺D

(INSTR) 1 | 1/7 6 6/5 | 4 5/5 | 4 3 | 5⁻ˢᵘˢ 5 ;)

⊘ S.

(TAG + Fade) 𝄆 1 | 1/7 6- 6-/5 | 4 3 | 5⁻ˢᵘˢ 5 ;) 𝄇

CHART: LARRY PAXTON

PAX

(G) 1 2 x x | 2 1 6⁴ˣ 4# 6⁴# | 5 | 1 3⁶ 4⁶ | 1 6 5 5 1/2
  4x4 shuffle

(C) = | 1 3 4 | 1 . 2 5 | 1 4 | 1 5 |
(V) = | 1 3 4 | 1 . 2 5 | 1 4 | 1 5 |
(C) = | 1 3 4 | 1 . 2 5 | 1 4 | 1 5 |
   Solo 𝄇

‡x ‡x

(V) = | 1 3 4 | 1 . 2 5 | 1 4 | 1 5 |
(C) = | 1 3 4 | 1 . 2 5 | 1 4 | 1 6 6 6 5 |

(TAG) 8 | 4# 3 2 4# 5↑ | 1 1 2 3 4 5 6 7 |
                        (Scale!)

1 6 5 3 | 1 5 1 -

STAND - REECE WYNANS

[F]

INTRO	5	1	♭7 4	1 7 4	1 7 4 5 ♭7
(CH)		1	4	1 ♭7/3 6-5 3-4	4 3- 4 ♭7 3-4
V)		5 6-	1 ♭6 4 1 ♭7 4		
(CH)		1	4	1	4 3-
V)		5 6-	1 4 1 4	6-5 3-4	4 6 3-4
(CH)		1	4	1	4 3-
Lick		1 2 7 4	5 ♭3 4	1 7 4	2 4 5
BR)		1	5 ♭3 4	♭3 6- ♭5 6-	5 ♭7 6 ♭7
(CH)		1	4	1	4 3- 5 7
					4 3- RIT

Intro: 1 5 4 1 6-5 1 1

V: 1 5 4 1 6-5 1 1   1 5 4 1 6-5 1 1

CH: 1 5 4 1 6-5 1 1

(C) 6-5 5-9 9 6 7 6 7 4 4 1 1 4 7 1 1

1 7 4 1 1

Instr: 1 5 4 1 6-5 1 1   1 5 4 1 6-5 1 1

6-5 5-9 9 7 7 6 7 6 7 4 1 1 1 4 7 1 1

Tag: 1 1 1 4 6 6 6 1 1 1 1 1   1 — 1

D.S. al coda

128

CHART: TROY LANCASTER

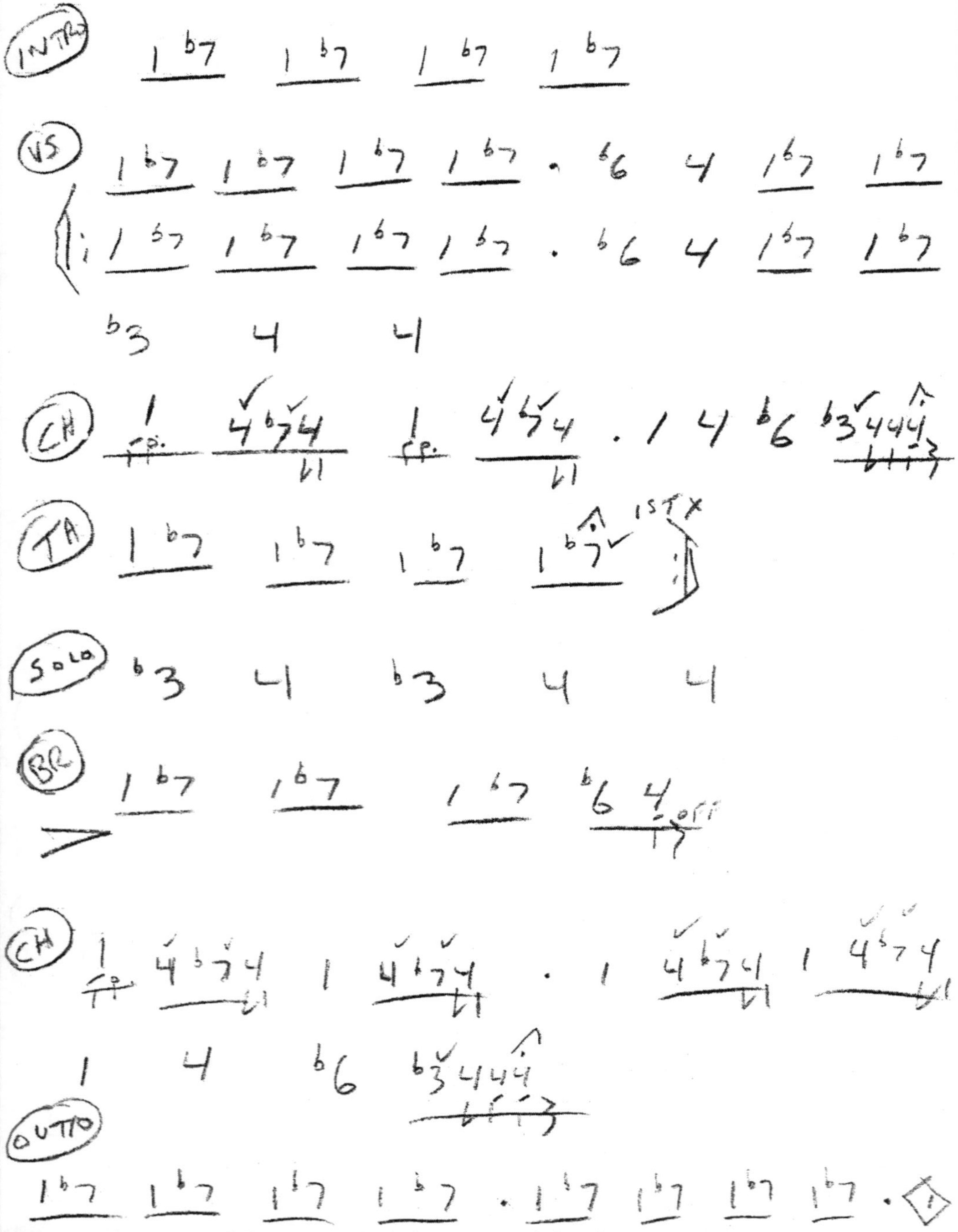

CHART: PAUL SCHOLTEN

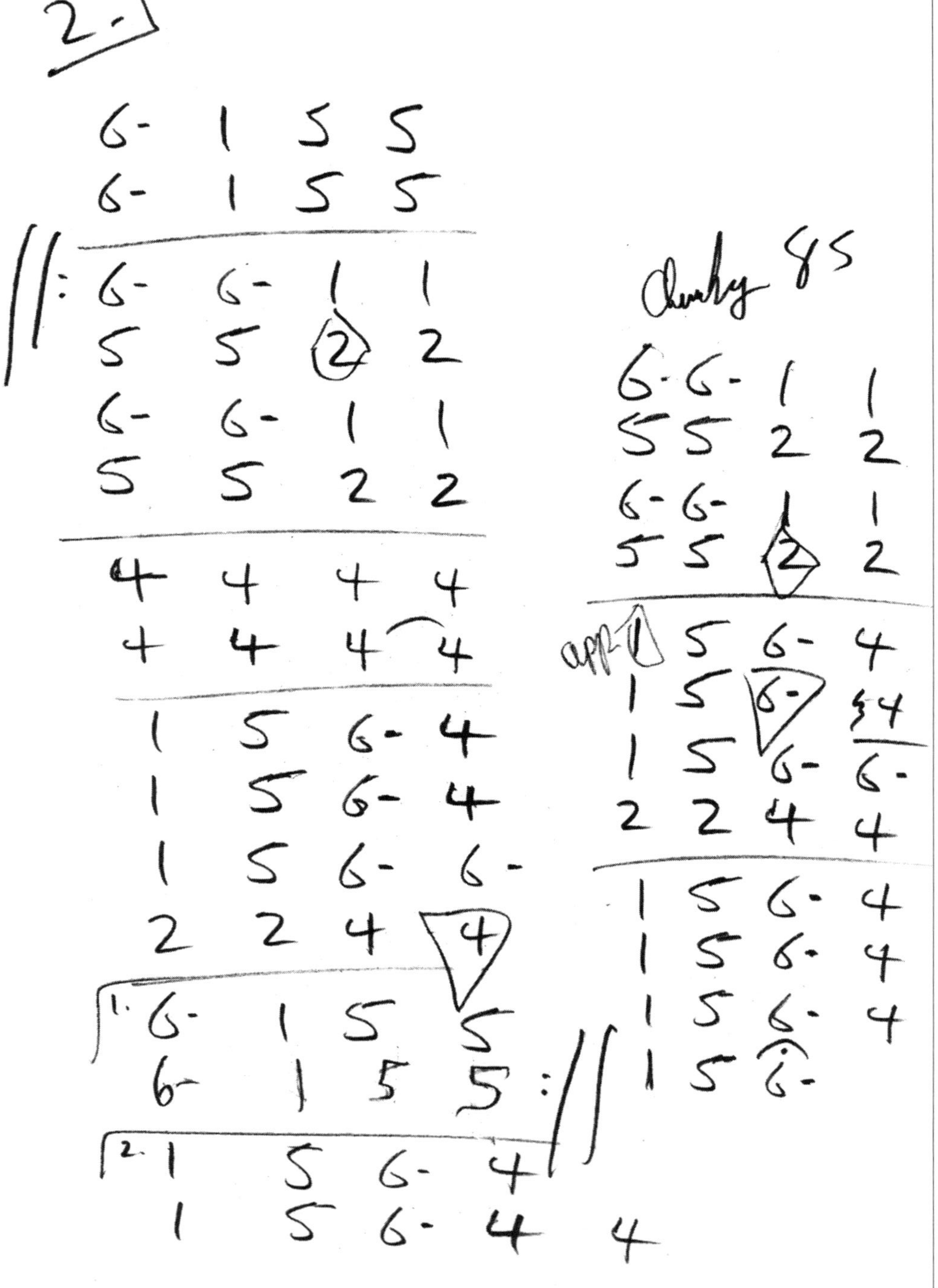

References:

Arnie Berle's Complete Handbook For Jazz Improvisation. Amsco Music Publishing Co.
A Modern Method For Guitar, Vol. I&II by William Leavitt. Berklee Press Publications.
Essential Dictionary of Music Notation by Tom Grou & Linda Lusk. Alfred Publishing Co.
Pocket Music Theory by Keith Wyatt & Carl Schroeder. Hal Leonard Corporation
www.allmusic.com

Thanks to:

Andy Most, Jeff King and all my friends who helped me with their musical knowledge and contributed their charts.

Ron de la Vega, who gave me the idea for the chapter on Speaking the Number System.
Ric Simenson at Computer Music Services for help with this typesetting software.
Rob Solberg at BrainWave Studios for building the cd rom.
Harrianne Condra at Sony/Tree for permission to use their songs in Editions 1-6.

And Thanks to all the musicians who were generous with their time telling me about the Nashville Number System and their experiences in the music business, as well as contributing their charts: Neal Matthews, Charlie McCoy, David Briggs, Brent Rowan, Lura Foster, Biff Watson, John Hobbs, Eddie Bayers, Jimmy Capps, Tony Harrell, Mike Chapman, Chris Farren, Wayne Moss, Bob Moore, Harold Bradley, Ray Edenton, Pete Wade, Weldon Myrick, Buddy Spicher, Barry Beckett, Brent Mason, Bob Patin, Jim Brown, Dann Huff, Randy Scruggs, Danny Parks, Paul Scholten, Dave Pomeroy, Troy Lancaster, Reese Wynans, Andy Most, Larry Paxton, Kerry Marx, Jeff King, Jim Hoke, Paul Leim, Bruce Bouton.

Website:
Please visit the NNS Website and let me know what you think about all this stuff:
www.nashvillenumbersystem.com